Also by Lisa Daily

Stop Getting Dumped!
All you need to know to make men fall madly in love
with you and marry "The One" in three years or less

Fifteen Minutes of Shame
A novel

"Not only is Lisa Daily absolutely hilarious, but she gives the best advice! Read, laugh, enjoy, but also do what she suggests because her advice is spot on!"
—Jennifer Muscato, *E! News*

"Confidence is sexy. Confidence plus knowledge—irresistible. Lisa Daily gives you both in her fast-paced, entertaining guide to dating over forty. Witty and smart, it's a must-read for any woman ready to find Mr. Right. Or at least Mr. Right Now."
—Christopher Hopkins, Oprah's Makeover Guy and author of *Staging Your Comeback: A Complete Beauty Revival for Women Over 45*

"This book is for every woman who's come to the realization, *This is a different world, I'm a different person, and I'm not doing things the same old way.*"
—Lisa Earle McLeod, *Buffalo News* syndicated columnist and author of *Finding Grace When You Can't Even Find Clean Underwear*

"No one knows dating like Lisa Daily, relationship guru extraordinaire. Lisa's the best at straight talk and honest answers. *How to Date Like a Grown-Up* is the bible for any woman thrust into the singles world either by choice or by circumstance."
—Jenny Gardiner, bestselling author of *Sleeping with Ward Cleaver*

"Lisa Daily is laugh out loud funny. Her writing is like sitting with a good girlfriend over drinks—honest, funny, and always memorable."
—Eileen Cook, author of *Unpredictable.*

"Funny, smart, compulsively readable. It's the book I would give a girlfriend in a second because it reads like the best kind of girlfriend advice."
—Gail Konop-Baker, author of *Cancer is a Bitch (Or, I'd Rather Be Having a Midlife Crisis.)*

"Once again Lisa Daily brings calm to a chaotic world. Her energetic, friendly voice cuts through the nonsense and brings fun back to dating for women already overwhelmed with the stresses of work, family, and changing health."
—Heidi Godman, ABC News (Health Reporter—Tampa/Sarasota)

"Lisa Daily cuts through the usual bull with smart, funny advice that works. *How to Date Like a Grown-Up* offers one-stop shopping for those in search of a meaningful relationship."
—Michael Alvear, star of HBO's *Sex Inspectors* and author of *Men Are Pigs But We Love Bacon*

"A must-read for all single grown-ups! In *How To Date Like a Grown-Up*, Lisa Daily dispenses excellent, no-nonsense advice for navigating the world of dating with confidence, grace, style, and a sense of humor."
—Danielle Younge-Ullman, author of *Falling Under*

How to Date Like a Grown-Up

How to Date Like a Grown-Up

*Everything You Need to Know to Get Out There,
Get Lucky, or Even Get Married in
Your 40s, 50s, and Beyond*

LISA DAILY

SOURCEBOOKS CASABLANCA™
AN IMPRINT OF SOURCEBOOKS, INC.®
NAPERVILLE, ILLINOIS

Published by Sourcebooks Casablanca, an imprint of Sourcebooks, Inc.
P.O. Box 4410, Naperville, Illinois 60567–4410
(630) 961–3900
Fax: (630) 961–2168
www.sourcebooks.com

Library of Congress Cataloging-in-Publication Data

Daily, Lisa.
  How to date like a grown-up : everything you need to know to get out there, get lucky, or even get married in your 40s, 50s, and beyond / Lisa Daily.
    p. cm.
  1. Middle-aged women—Psychology. 2. Dating (Social customs) 3. Man-woman relationships. I. Title.
  HQ1059.4.D35 2008
  646.7'7082—dc22
                              2008034034

Printed and bound in the United States of America.
BG 10 9 8 7 6 5 4 3 2 1

To Mom, Tom, Elle, and Quinn.
And every woman who has ever suffered
through a bad date.

Contents

Introduction

It's a Lot Easier to Date Once Your Eyesight Starts to Go

Raise your hand if you've ever been on a date so bad that halfway through the calamari you were thinking, *Why in the world am I still sitting here listening to this guy? Stabbing myself in the arm with a fork or attending a four-day seminar on putting paper clips up my nose would be more interesting.*

When you were twenty, or even thirty, you probably would have forced yourself to sit through the entire date, hoping it would get better, making an effort to make some sort of human connection with this person, or digging for something—anything—you might be able to use to piece together an intelligent conversation.

Now, you're just not interested in wasting an entire evening on a date that's going nowhere.

A lot of things change once we hit forty.

I'm not just talking about those silver hairs that begin to sprout overnight, or those little tiny wrinkles around your eyes that weren't there yesterday, or the fact that you probably shouldn't go braless ever again. (Even if they still are fabulous, you probably want to give them all the help you can.)

In your twenties and thirties, you're looking outside yourself—you're trying to accomplish things, kick-start your career, define yourself. By the time you hit forty, you finally have a pretty good idea of who you are, and that changes everything.

You're a grown-up, which means you're looking for something more when it comes to dating, love, and romance.

You want love, companionship, commitment, sex. Sometimes you want all of those things wrapped up in one fabulous package. Sometimes you just want one or the other: romance à la carte.

You are tired of waiting for the right guy to show up, and yet, you're still hopeful that he will. Which is why the usual "head-out-to-the-bar-and-meet-your-Prince-Charming" book aimed at twenty-somethings just isn't going to cut it for you.

Why Dating Like a Grown-Up Is Different

This book will tell you everything you need to know to get back out into the dating world after a long marriage or dating hiatus, how to have better luck (or meet better men) if you've been on the dating scene for a while, how to just get lucky, or how to get married if that's what you're looking for. *How to Date Like a Grown-Up* will teach you the best (and worst) places to meet men; reveal what forty-, fifty-, and sixty-year-old women have that their twenty- and thirty-year-old counterparts don't; and let you in on all of the places and situations that might be making you a magnet for losers.

Want to Get Out There?

I'll tell you how to avoid feeling like the invisible woman; where to find the best untapped places to meet nice, decent, and attractive men; how to deal with the pitfalls and benefits of dating younger men; and whether or not it's a good idea to try to rekindle an old flame. I'll clue you in on the methods of the new pick-up artists so you can spot the men who are just looking for a quick romp (whether this is a good thing or not is your call). I'll give you some little-known secrets that will improve your dating odds dramatically and teach you how to work a room. I'll help you learn how to sift through the jerks, prisoners, and married men online; teach you a foolproof method for picking an online dating site that best meets your needs; and show you why speed dating can be the most time-efficient dating method under the sun. You'll also learn how to break it to your kids that your social life is more interesting than theirs is. (Read this book, and I promise it will be!)

Want to Get Lucky?

You're not the only one. I'll let you know when to avoid a one-night (or ten-night) stand and when to go for it, how to tell if a man is just looking for sex, and how to face getting naked in front of someone new for the first time. I'll tell you what men really think about sleeping with women over forty, how to accommodate changes in your body (and his), and explain the good and bad of the little blue pill.

What's more, I'll clue you in on the one thing you can do in the bedroom to make a man speed up his marriage proposal.

Want to Get Married?

I'll let you know why men over forty are rushing to the altar and, for once, why many women are holding back. You'll learn the skinny on living together versus getting married and the financial considerations for both.

I'll help you navigate the etiquette for second- or third-time brides and first-time brides over forty. And I'll throw in some pointers from experts on how to gracefully handle children, stepchildren, exes, and other assorted relatives on your big day.

If You've Got Questions About Dating Like a Grown-Up, I Can Help

I'm Lisa Daily, and for six years I've been helping women change their lives and attract the kind of men they've been searching for. I am a dating coach, columnist, and the relationship expert on *Daytime*, a syndicated morning TV show. During the last two years, I have interviewed hundreds of men and women over forty about what they're looking for in a relationship as well as what they're looking to avoid. I've learned where they're looking (and where the good ones are hiding), what works, and what doesn't. I've answered hundreds of viewer and reader letters and received thousands more. (You'll see many of them throughout the book.) I've interviewed dozens of experts in a variety of fields, read hundreds of studies, and even conducted a survey, the Grown-Up Dating Survey, specifically for this book.

I want to help you get from here to happily ever after.

The Grown-Up Dating Survey

In 2008 we conducted a survey of three hundred daters over the age of forty to learn what they're looking for in a date or a relationship, the success they've had with various dating methods, and the surprising things that can make or break a relationship.

You'll find the fascinating results throughout this book.

When my book *Stop Getting Dumped! All You Need to Know to Make Men Fall Madly in Love with You and Marry "The One" in 3 Years or Less* was published, I began teaching a class called the Dreamgirl Academy all across the country. I expected that the women who attended would be in their early twenties and thirties, and many were—but many, sometimes more than half, were in their forties, fifties, and sixties.

It was a scenario that played out over and over again, at signings, seminars, and speaking engagements from L.A. to New York. After each event, women would wait for me, buying books and lingering to ask questions and share the challenges they faced in dating: *Where do you go to meet men if you wouldn't be caught dead in a bar? What do you do if the last time you had sex was ten years ago? Don't men just want to date twenty-year-olds?* Their questions and issues weren't answered or even addressed in the glut of dating-advice books targeting twenty- and thirty-somethings.

Sometimes, I'd end up staying to talk for an hour or more. It was clear that what these amazing women had in common with my younger readers was that they too wanted to love and be loved. But while their maturity, in many cases, had given them a new confidence, it also brought with it a whole new set of insecurities and challenges: a secret, gnawing part of us worries that our bodies and our baggage keep us from measuring up to a twenty-six-year-old with flat abs.

My job, and the job of this book, is to give you the answers you're looking for and, most importantly, to show you how amazing you are and why you don't have to worry about competing with perky breasts and unwrinkled skin. I'll show you why you're in a whole different league.

5 Reasons Why You're Fabulous but Dateless

1. **You live in New York City**. An article in the February 2007 issue of *National Geographic* states that there are 180,000 more single women than men in the NYC area. See, it's not you—it's your city! Don't you feel better?

2. **You have young children**. Unfair as it is, here's the reality you're working with: statistically speaking, single moms have a harder time dating than their childless counterparts. Does that mean you're doomed to spinsterhood? No. It just means you'll have to date a little smarter.

3. **You smoke**. Men and women over forty are more health conscious. In fact, 86 percent of respondents in the Grown-Up Dating Survey said the issue of smoking was "very important" or "somewhat important."

4. **You got screwed in your divorce**. If you're still hanging on to some anger over your divorce, you're going to repel any decent guy who crosses your path. I'm sorry you had to go through that terrible experience. Now, make yourself an appointment with a counselor or a manicurist and get it all out, darlin'. Otherwise, you'll be going through that terrible experience for the rest of your life.

5. **You make over $100,000**. Bad news, ladies: once you hit a certain income level, you actually start repelling men. You have two choices here: be coquettish about your finances until after the engagement, or put it all out there and date a more secure, albeit smaller, pool of men. If you take my advice, be yourself. He's going to find out you're a rock star sooner or later. It might as well be now.

Part 1

Get Out There

Chapter 1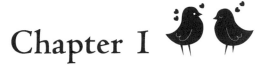

It's Not Easy Being the Invisible Woman

I remember the first time that no one rushed to my rescue when I struggled to put a suitcase in the overhead compartment on an airplane.

It was a shock. Men, for as long as I could remember, had always offered to hoist my bag into the overhead compartment, open doors, carry boxes to my car, and surrender their taxis to me. Truth be told, I sort of considered it my birthright, a testament to my obvious charm or inherent fabulousness (don't we all do that?).

And it wasn't as if there were no men on the plane. There were just no men who had watched me walk down the aisle and waited for an opening.

I was traveling alone, about six months after my daughter was born, which meant I was frumpier, ten pounds heavier than my usual, and obviously sleep-deprived (at least that's what I was saying to delude myself into believing that those bags under my eyes were only temporary). In my defense, I was not looking my best. But the incident highlighted something that had been creeping up, something that I hadn't really noticed until that moment.

I had become invisible.

I'm not really sure when it happened exactly, so I can't be positive if I'd crossed some unseen line of reproductive viability or if it was caused by something more tangible, like a mass email sent out on a random Thursday in March to inform the male species that I was officially off the hit list. But it was clear that the attention from male strangers that I had taken for granted all my life—that same attention I had frequently found tiresome or irritating to endlessly fend off—had suddenly slowed down to a trickle.

After the airplane incident, I was suddenly more aware of the men who *didn't* try to catch my eye at the gas station, at the grocery store, at the beach.

I did notice that I seemed to be a lot more attractive on Fridays, which is the day I tape my TV segment, when I'm dressed to the nines with my hair blown out and significantly more makeup than I wear in my normal life.

Men are a lot more likely to flirt with me on Fridays.

Now, I'm not saying you need to spend an hour and a half getting ready to walk out the door in the morning, but I can tell you, it does make a perceptible difference. If you look better, you feel better, and more men *pay attention.*

I also noticed that while I got significantly less "*woo-hoo, hey baby, what are you doing later?*" attention from construction workers, bar letches, and the general male population than in my earlier years, the attention that I did get was more focused. The men who flirted with me did so because they'd discovered some common interest, because they were curious about what I'd accomplished, because I was funny, or because they were interested in talking to me, in hearing what I had to say.

So yes, the bad news is that at some point, the male interest doesn't come as quickly.

But the good news is that when men do notice you, it's based on something a lot more substantial. They are, *gasp*, actually interested in getting to know you, in your mind, in your *opinions*.

So while the sheer numbers may have gone down, the odds of meeting someone you have something in common with, someone you might actually want to get to know better, have actually gone up.

As off-putting as it may be to realize you're not the hottest young thing in the room anymore, we should all be deliriously happy about the fact that when we're holding court with a group of men at a party or meeting, it's because they're actually interested in what we have to say.

Which, if you ask me, is a lot more compelling than someone who's only interested in the possibility of seeing you naked.

Because the men who are interested in your brain first, well, they want to see you naked too.

Twenty, Thirty, Forty, Fifty, and Fabulous

This realization—that you've reached a certain point—is upsetting for a lot of women.

Well, crap, they think. *I'm OLD. How in the world am I going to compete with some twenty-six-year-old with perky boobs and no baggage?*

You're not. And it's not because you can't; it's because you don't need to.

You don't need to compete with those women. You are now operating on a whole different plane.

Yes, some men are looking for twenty-six-year-olds. But those are not the men you want to date. Besides, squeezing yourself into a boob tube and stilettos to go hang out at the local watering hole isn't going to fool anyone, right?

At least not close up. Or before midnight.

And that's okay.

It's time to think about the things that really make you attractive.

You Know Who You Are

A grown-up is not looking for a man to define who she is. If anything, the men you date will have to find a way to fit into *your* life.

You Have Your Own Life

A grown-up is not going to dump all of her friends to hang out with some guy or remake her life to better match his. You have a career; you have friends; you have a home; and you have stuff to do.

You've Seen a Few Things

From dating partners with trouble getting it up to witnessing 9/11, a woman with more life experience has an easier time putting things in perspective. If the worst thing that ever happened to you is a two-year waiting list for a handbag, you're far more likely to freak out over the fact that your guy has just been restructured out of a job or some equally troubling but non-life-threatening occurrence. Internally, you've got a sharper compass.

You're Comfortable with Sex

This may come as a shock, but women in their forties have far fewer hang-ups about sex than their twenty-year-old counterparts do. (I know, I know, how many of your friends have said, "I wish I took more pictures of myself in a bikini—I had no idea how fabulous/skinny/blonde I was back then.") There's a reason that young men fantasize about sex with an older woman (more about that in Chapter 4!). You're more adventurous and less likely to worry about your body, about the little mishaps and noises that happen in bed, and you're far less likely to give a crap about what he'll think of you in the morning. Which means you're more likely to just let loose and have fun. And there's nothing sexier than that.

"Women over forty have been looking at their bodies for decades, for better or for worse. After a while, they realize that there is more to life than worrying about a little jiggle on the thigh area."
—Jeanne B.

You're Secure Enough Not to Waste Time with Someone Who Isn't a Good Fit

While younger women spend months or years with inappropriate men, by the time you hit forty, you're all done messing around.

You've Got Your Childbearing Issues Pretty Much Worked Out

At this stage of the game, you either have kids, don't want them, or you're working on a husband-free parenting plan. For most men over forty, the fact that this issue is resolved for you makes you a more appealing candidate for a relationship.

You're Less Inclined to Wig Out If Things Go Wrong

With age comes maturity and the ability to take a breath before you start hurling china. Grown-ups understand that screaming matches aren't sport. Men, who seek to avoid drama like the bird flu, are appreciative of a woman who doesn't flip out, shriek, threaten to leave, or set his clothes on fire in the driveway when the two of you don't see eye to eye. You react in a way that's much more reasonable.

Men's Thoughts on Women Over 40

"What makes women over forty attractive is their lower expectations, wisdom, relatability, and tolerability of imperfection. They're not as high maintenance as younger women still struggling with the princess syndrome."
—Paul Davis (love coach)

"As a fifty-one-year-old man who has done some dating over the past decade, I can tell you the best thing about dating women over forty is that you really know what you're getting off the bat . . . or at least by the second date. There's less game playing—if the woman is a gold digger, you know it; if she doesn't like you, she'll generally tell you. Some guys may find this difficult, but I'd rather know what I'm in for right away, rather than have a younger woman 'play' me for a while until the right man comes along. Last March, I met the woman of my dreams, and I knew it from the minute I saw her. We're getting married on March 19, a year to the day we met. Never a doubt in my mind, and she's forty-seven."

—Wayne Schaffel (president of a public relations firm)

"What makes women over forty attractive is, quite simply, who they have become and who they are becoming, which captures others' attention because of their looks, humor, depth, insight, and experience."
—Dion McInnis (photographer)

"Confidence in who you are is always attractive to men who are sure of themselves. Men who are less sure of themselves seek the 'trophy,' as opposed to the brain."
—Mark Amtower (author)

Letters to Lisa

Dear Lisa,

I met this guy online, and he seemed perfect. We got into each other maybe a little too fast. The week we ended our correspondence, I sensed something was wrong. I asked him about it, and he said he and his ex were fighting and it really bothered him. He said maybe this was bad timing, but he felt as though he should pull out before things with us got too serious. Unfortunately, it was too late for me; now all I can think about is him.

Should I try to contact him or let it go?

Functional Keyboard, Broken Heart

Dear Functional,

Let him go, sweetie. He still has feelings for his ex, and he's trying to let you down easy. It's easy to wonder "what if" in this situation, but it won't get him over his ex any faster, and it will wind up making you crazy. Move forward with your life. You deserve to be with someone who is able and available to love you.

Best,

Lisa

Fear Factor

One of the things that happen as we get older and more experienced is that it becomes more difficult to just enjoy a date as a date. We don't want to waste time; we're savvy enough to have made some mistakes; and we go into the first-date experience bound and determined to make an assessment as to the gentleman's final mate potential before the appetizers arrive.

For women, dating mistakes like these are based in fear. Fear we won't get married before our eggs dry up. Fear someone wants us only for our money. Fear that someone might try to deceive or hurt us. And that fear is what keeps any of us from being happy, and, ultimately, finding what we want.

The secret to love, of course, is that in order to find it, you have to let go of the terror that you'll end up a puddle when the whole deal is done. Which means that it's probably a good idea to stop trying to hog-tie Cupid; relax and put your faith in the universe, God, Buddha, corporate America, or whatever else you believe in. Trust that there's someone out there just for you, and just let it happen.

You deserve to be loved, and there is someone in the world (probably several someones, actually) who is up to the task.

Let's figure out where to find him.

Chapter 2

31 Surefire Secrets to Improve Your Dating Odds

Real Beauty Is on the Inside... But the Outside Is Kinda Important, Too

Let's talk about why it's important to take care of yourself and look as good as you possibly can.

The quickest and easiest way to feel good is to look good. If you feel good about yourself, you're less likely to settle for anyone who doesn't treat you like the amazing, fabulous person you are. When we look good, we feel more confident; we walk a little taller; we feel stronger; and we attract other confident, successful, and happy people to us.

When we feel miserable or fat or vulnerable or unfulfilled, we tend to attract people who don't have our best interests at heart.

Sure, it may be comfy to run to the grocery store, the gas station, and the dry cleaner in sweatpants and a scrunchie, but this is not the way to bring out your inner confidence. First, you never know whom you might meet. (And trust me, you're far more likely to run into every single one of your neighbors or that great-looking guy from your office on the one occasion you go out with dirty hair and a raincoat over your pajamas.)

Second, when you're pumping gas and happen to catch your own reflection in the window, if you look like crap, you're not going to feel nearly as good as when you catch yourself looking spectacular.

The truth is, many psychologists agree that the care you take with your appearance is usually a reflection of how you feel about yourself, and sometimes those two things are more closely tied than we might imagine. In my own experience with the women I coach, I see that the happier women are with their lives, the more effort they take with how they look.

But sometimes we wake up and don't recognize ourselves in the mirror.

Maybe you gave up everything important that wasn't related to your children (career, girlfriend time, grown-up conversations, pedicures, Sundays at the art museum, and going to the bathroom all by yourself) and found yourself fast-forwarded eight years, twenty pounds, and three thousand macaroni-and-cheese dinners later, wondering where the "real" you went.

Maybe you've been stuck in a job that sucks the life out of you.

Maybe you've spent the last five years in a marriage in which no one really cared how you looked anyway, so why bother?

It's a vicious cycle: we feel bad, so we don't want to bother with how we look, and then the worse we look, the worse we feel. Repeat.

Conversely, psychologists have found that taking time with your appearance can actually help jog you out of a self-esteem low.

Why? Because you're making the effort to care about yourself.

I always tell women: You can't expect a man to pamper you if you won't even do it for yourself.

Start today.

Treat yourself to a bubble bath or a pedicure or a massage or a facial (or if you have the time and the money, all of the above) every week. Do whatever it is that makes you feel and look your best.

Keys to Looking Fabulous Over 40

Tip #1:

Get a great haircut and maintain it.

Tip #2:

Moisturize.

Tip #3:

Pluck, wax, or shape your eyebrows on a regular basis (even if they're starting to thin out a bit—waxing them into shape will actually make them look thicker and less "spready").

Tip #4:

Eliminate anything from your wardrobe that doesn't flatter your figure and your coloring.

Tip #5:

Whiten your teeth—it's easy, relatively cheap, and can take YEARS off your life. If your teeth have been bonded and the material has begun to yellow, try using the whitening gel on the back side of your teeth, where it can penetrate.

Tip #6:

Exercise three times a week. (I'm a fan of the T-Tapp workout— www.t-tapp.com. It really whittles down your waist, and my skin has never looked better.) Plus, exercise releases all kinds of happy endorphins in your brain, so you'll look better *and* feel better.

Tip #7:

Eat more veggies.

Tip #8:

Invest in a pair of Spanx, and stop fretting about everything else.

Tip #9:

Take your vitamins—including fish oil.

Tip #10:

Switch to dark chocolate.

Tip #11:

Make a list of your five best features, and do everything you can to play them up.

Tip #12:

Quit obsessing about everything else.

Tip #13:

Do something that nourishes your soul, whether it's helping out at your church, taking photographs, or planting tomatoes. We feel happier and more beautiful when we're doing something spiritual.

> Most men don't expect you to look like a supermodel. They just want to feel like you made a little effort.

Should You Wash That Gray Right Out of Your Hair?

Sometimes it happens at twenty-three; sometimes it doesn't happen until fifty-five. But most of us have spotted a gray or two (or fifty-seven) on occasion. For many women, the idea of going gray feels old. Old lady. Old lady with cats. Blah.

So should you color or not?

Whether or not you decide to color your hair should depend on two things: how gray hair makes you feel, and how gray hair makes you look.

Writer Anne Kreamer chronicled her decision to stop dyeing her hair at forty-nine, after almost twenty-five years, in her fascinating book, *Going Gray: What I Learned about Beauty, Sex, Work, Motherhood, Authenticity, and Everything Else That Matters.* What I found particularly interesting was that Kreamer got more responses with her gray-haired online-dating profile on Match.com than she did with the exact same profile with her hair dyed brown. You can see before-and-after pictures of Anne and other women who've decided to go gray at her website, www.annekreamer.com.

Tip #14:

Your best bet is to sit down and have a hair-color heart-to-heart with three girlfriends and a stylist you trust. Before you make the switch, try on wigs, cut pictures out of *More* magazine, or upload your photo to www.thehairstyler.com, where you can see virtually what you'd look like with different hair colors.

How to Work a Room Like an Expert

Okay, so now you're looking fabulous; you're feeling good; and your new (or maybe your old) hair color is in order. Now it's time to go out and shake it around a bit. Whether you're going to a work function, a date, or heading out to your first speed-dating function, the last thing you want to do is fade into the woodwork. Use the tips experts recommend below to get the attention you deserve, no matter where you go.

Here's how the grown-up dater works it.

Tip #15: Front and Center

According to spatial psychologists, if you want to attract attention, you should be standing in the center of the room and moving around a bit (think more "exuding energy" and less "flapping like a chicken").

If you're in a bar or nightclub, you'll get the most action at the corners on the bar. Why? It's easier to talk to someone when you're at a ninety-degree angle versus lined up like monkeys on the flat side of the bar. So not only will you meet more people, but according to studies done by spatial psychologist Dr. Albert Mehrabian, bartenders tend to gravitate toward the corners as well. (Good to know if you're ever waiting for a refill on your chocolatini.) Interesting conversation *and* a full drink? Sounds like a fabulous night to me.

The worst place to attract attention is hanging out near the wall or sitting alone at a table. Handsome strangers approach your table and ask, "May I join you?" only in cheesy movies. If you've got a book with you, you might as well have a sign on your forehead that says Please Don't Bother Me.

Tip #16: Red for Sex, Pink for Love

Did you know that certain colors can make you more or less appealing to the opposite sex?

According to Leatrice Eiseman, director of the Pantone Color Institute, women should wear a soft pinky-peach to make themselves most approachable. The color is "very flattering to most skin tones; it gives you a healthy glow," and, according to Eiseman, projects "a little vulnerability, which brings out something protective in men."

Want to wear a color that weeds out guys who can't handle strong women? (Who doesn't?!) Try a deep red, burgundy, or plum. Men who aren't attracted to strong women will steer clear, which will save you the trouble of having to stomp on their hearts with your stilettos on the way out the door.

Of all the colors, red is the most sensual, but wear red with caution. Red adds an element of excitement and attracts two types of guys—men interested primarily in sex and men attracted to powerful women. (I know, I know, you're thinking, *um, aren't all men interested in sex?* Yes—but I'm talking about attracting the ones who are *only* interested in sex.) So yes, if you choose to wear red, you may have to fend off a lot of freaks, but you could also end up meeting a man who isn't threatened by the fact that you make a bigger salary. Also, red is the perfect color to add a little *vroom vroom* to an already established relationship.

If you're worried that your wardrobe might be driving the men away, steer clear of what Eiseman calls "squished-caterpillar yellow-green," which apparently repels both men *and* women.

And if you'd like to be able to spot the nice guys in a crowd right away, keep an eye out for the men in blue. According to Eiseman, guys who frequently wear blue are "stable, faithful, constant, and always there." The blue guy is a fantastic candidate for a long-term relationship—he's dependable, monogamous, and best of all, he can match his own clothes.

Tip #17: Be Fluent in Body Language

The key to using body language to attract the opposite sex is in making yourself as approachable as possible.

Basically, you want to send the guy a message that he won't get shot down immediately if he tries to spark a conversation with you. Otherwise, he may never get the nerve up to try.

First, avoid folding your arms, and don't chew on gum, ice, or your fingernails. Body-language experts say that the chewing indicates anxiety, frustration, or general unrest—none of which are very attractive emotions.

According to body-language expert Patti Wood, you want to make yourself a "safe" (read "approachable") target. How do you accomplish that?

Don't take up a lot of space (which, in body-language terms, is a sign of power and superiority), and keep your stance feminine (feet less than six inches apart, toes turned slightly inward) and your posture relaxed. According to Wood, "We are strong women, but remember, we're trying to get a man to come over and talk to us." She explains, "You have to show you have room for someone else in your life."

Tip #18: Smile—the Instant Facelift

Psychology and body-language experts agree that one of the most important things you can do to make yourself more attractive (and approachable) is to smile. It's the quickest, easiest way to improve your looks—no surgery or effort required.

Tip #19: Smells Like Love

Studies at the University of Chicago showed that men associate the scents of cinnamon and vanilla with love. (Cinnamon buns, pumpkin pie, doughnuts, and lavender were the top scents to get men in the mood for love). Cheese pizza and buttered popcorn also did the trick.

To make the scents work for you, try baking some ready-made cinnamon rolls about an hour before your date arrives, or wear a cinnamon-vanilla scented perfume (there's a fabulous one that was created just for me called Man Magnet at www. chooseherbs.com).

Why does it work? Aromatherapy experts have long believed cinnamon to be an aphrodisiac. According to Laura Davimes, aromatherapy expert and owner of Herban Avenues, "Certain aromatic plants exude oils similar to our own sexual secretions or pheromones. Wearing cinnamon-vanilla blends increases the presence of pheromone-like substances and dramatically increases attraction." Another possibility is that the scents of popcorn, cinnamon rolls, pumpkin pie, and the like might trigger feelings of security, comfort, and good times, which can put us in a more relaxed mood.

How to Look Fabulous on a First Date

Of course I want you to *look* as spectacular as you are, so I asked for some advice from my friend Christopher Hopkins, the Makeover Guy seen on *Oprah* and author of *Staging Your Comeback: A Complete Beauty Revival for Women Over 45.* (If you're looking to give your image an overhaul or even just a tweak, I highly recommend it.)

Below, you'll find Christopher's top tips for how to look your best on a first date.

Tip #20:

First choice: candlelight.

Tip #21:

In daylight, sit with the window behind you to create a "halo effect."

Tip #22:

You can always "slip into something more comfortable," but until then, Spanx and the high-impact bra.

Tip #23:

Soft lips, perfume, and a little cleavage are timelessly seductive.

Tip #24:

Check it out from behind, head to toe, with a rear-view mirror before you leave the house. He'll be watching you walk away. (See tip #22)

Flirty over Forty

So you've got your room-owning strategies in place, and all eyes are on you. What next?

Well, my dear, it's time to dust off the ol' flirting skills. You don't have to look like Angelina Jolie to make men take notice; all you really need is your fabulous smile and a few surefire flirting tips like the ones you'll find below. Now, pick out a charming man and get to work.

Tip #25: Lock Eyes

Lock eyes with the man you're flirting with for a full five to six seconds; then smile and drop your gaze. Don't stare a hole through the guy's forehead, for goodness sake—just give him a smoldering, come-hither look, and look away. Do this at least three times in a ten- to fifteen-minute period. Why? He needs to know it's him you're flirting with, and eye contact is a universal signal of openness.

Tip #26: Be a Vampire's Best Friend

One of the most winning flirting techniques a woman can use is the exposure of her neck. This can be done with a head tilt to one side, the classic hair flip, or my personal favorite, the over-the-shoulder glance—the asymmetrical position attracts attention, exposes your neck, and gives you the opportunity to lock eyes. The over-the-shoulder move is extra effective, because it's sexy and it sends a signal to your target that he is worth a second look. And maybe a third.

Tip #27: How's Your Hair?

We tend to preen or groom ourselves subconsciously when we're attracted to someone by smoothing down our hair or clothes or checking our lipstick in a compact. Men will generally smooth their hair, pull up their socks, or straighten their ties. Try combining a grooming gesture with a smile and a gaze. Another trick? Toss your hair to one side. This classic move is a double whammy that combines preening and a flash of neck. Need I say more?

Tip #28: Cross Your Legs

Crossing and uncrossing your legs is another effective flirting technique, especially if you're wearing high heels. (Although, don't overuse this one—you don't want to give the impression that you're about to have a bathroom emergency.) The act of crossing your legs is quite seductive to men, and it makes them hungry to see more. Another key seduction trick is slipping your heel out of your shoe and dangling it on your toes. The arch of the foot sends a sexual message, mimics a woman's curves, and sends a man's heart racing. These particular flirting techniques are more obvious, so be sure to use them sparingly.

Tip #29: Be a Mimic

When people are attracted to each other, they mirror each other's body language with similar gestures, voice volume, etc. Try *subtly* mimicking the man's behavior. If he leans forward, you lean forward. If he scratches his head, you scratch your head. If you are mirroring someone's behavior, they'll begin to feel as though the two of you are connected and in tune with each other. The key is to be subtle. The last thing you want is to give off a "monkey see, monkey do" vibe.

Tip #30: Focus, Focus, Focus

Once you and your guy have started talking, use these tips to lock in the attraction. First, smile and maintain eye contact as he is speaking, and focus all of your attention on what he is saying. (Yes, it's true: rarely is anyone more attractive than someone who finds you utterly fascinating.) Other key moves—the nod and the head tilt—signal you're listening to what the other person has to say. Smiling and laughing are crucial here also—it's the quickest, easiest way to put another person at ease and make a connection. Finally, another effective flirting technique is low-level touching, such as brushing the shoulder, elbow, or kneecap.

Tip #31: Is He Flashing You?

How can you tell if a man is flirting with you? The signs above are fantastic indicators, but men tend to take things a little further by demonstrating their social status with moves that can include flashing cash and talking about their careers and (you guessed it) cars.

Chapter 3

Mortuaries and Other Pick-Up Joints

Think Outside the Bar

Okay, ladies. It's time to get back out there in the world. If you want to meet someone, you're going to need to get off the couch. (Unless you hit it off with the cable repair guy—then you can just microwave yourself another bag of popcorn and sit right back down.) While you may be worried that all the good men are either married or dead, I'm here to tell you that there are some great guys out there who *are* worth your time.

It breaks my heart when I hear women and men say that there aren't any good ones left, because it's just not true. Sure, it *feels* true when you're sitting across the table from your blind date—a guy who wears black socks with sandals and whines about how his seventh divorce really was all *his wife's fault*, because frankly, in his opinion, all women are inherently evil, gold diggers, or both.

But there are a lot of decent men and women who are single and looking for someone to love: maybe they made a few mistakes in their first marriage; maybe they've never been married; or maybe the spouse they loved has passed away. I know this because I've met so many of you—men and women who are a little older, a little (or a lot) wiser, and still hoping to find someone to share a life with.

Yes, it's true there are lots of men who are damaged, depressed, and generally irritated about their past relationships. (And ladies, let's be fair here—the guys aren't the only ones hanging on to anger, hurt, and disappointment.) But there are also a lot of men and women out there who have learned from their mistakes, who want to find love and do better this time. That's not to mention the folks who had it pretty good the first time around and are looking for someone to love again.

So where do you go to meet these wonderful, enlightened, please-let-them-be-attractive, minimally damaged men and women?

We all know that once you hit your fortieth (er, thirtieth) birthday, you're not going to have much luck spending every weekend hanging out in a bar, gripping a bottle of light beer, listening to the same old jokes, and meeting the same people in different clothes. When we belly up to the bar, we're much more likely to meet that smarmy loser whose exposed silver chest hairs seem perilously likely to fall in our drinks than the man of our dreams.

That said, there are lots of great places to meet someone fabulous, and many of them have little or no competition.

Where are they? Well, girls, let me fill you in.

It's Ladies' Night at the Crematorium

Whether it's the passing of a neighbor's spouse, a close pal, or a friend's parent, funerals are the new wedding receptions for the over-forty crowd. This may seem a bit, um, morbid, but there are two reasons why funerals are actually a lovely spot to meet nice men. (And I'm not just talking about the widower.) First, it's a social gathering of lots of people your age—friends, family, and business associates. Second, if you're at the funeral in the first place, you probably knew and liked the deceased, or maybe you're friends with his or her children. (And no, I don't recommend crashing the funerals of strangers.) It's highly likely you'll be at least somewhat compatible with anyone who is friends with a good friend of yours. This is because we tend to choose friends with similar looks, education, and values to our own.

And if you happen to be one of those compassionate people who goes to a friend's mother's funeral because the friend is really worried that no one else will show up (maybe Mom was evil or crazy or just outlived all of her friends and family), know that you'll meet other, equally compassionate people there who know how important it is to be a good friend.

And while a widower is probably not going to be ready to hook up with a new flame ten minutes after the service (and you probably should avoid those who are), you can open the door by offering your support. People who are happily married and widowed have a very good chance at a successful second marriage.

And one more thing: keep an eye out for single pallbearers—they're probably reasonably fit and have some sense of duty and loyalty. All in all, not a bad start.

Your friend *would have wanted* you to be happy. Am I right?

How Long Should You Wait to Pounce on the Widower?

Widowed men tend to remarry fairly quickly (the long-accepted average is within about two and a half years). But it's pretty tacky to flirt with a gentleman at his wife's funeral. You want to let the poor guy have a little time to grieve. Give him two or three months to get his bearings back before you start angling for a date. And don't panic that you'll be missing your big chance—I know, I know, the widows in Buicks start lining up at the funeral parlor—but you want to distinguish yourself from the pack. These men are inundated after the funeral—it's casserole city. Give him a little space, and then make your move when the throng of ladies has thinned a bit. You'll come off as more genuine and less desperate than your tuna-surprise-wielding counterparts.

Go Clubbing

Want to meet an endless supply of fit, financially comfortable, educated men? Take up golf. Trust me, men go crazy for a woman who can swing a crooked stick. And once you start, you might just find you're as addicted to golf as the guys are.

If you don't already golf, there are lots of reasonably priced lessons at your local public course. (And of course, plenty of overpriced ones at the private clubs.)

Once you've mastered the basics, you have two options to maximize your man-meeting potential: You can pull together a foursome with a collection of like-minded women, or you can head out to the course on Saturday morning as a single and complete someone else's foursome.

If you bring your own foursome, most of your socializing will probably take place in the clubhouse after your round. And a group of four women in a clubhouse overpopulated by men is bound to stand out like a basket of daisies.

If you're golfing as a single, you'll be meeting three new people— most likely men—and odds are in your favor that at least one of them is single. (The Census Bureau estimates that 30 percent of

Americans born between 1946 and 1964 are single.) You'll have him all to yourself for eighteen holes, and if you like him, you can let him buy you a Bloody Mary when you finish your round.

Now, you might be thinking you'd rather golf with your married friends Barb and Frank, who are fun to hang with and who will certainly not roll their eyes when you hit your ball into the middle of the lake, like a bunch of strange men might.

However, if you're golfing out for the purpose of meeting other people, you'll be far less likely to socialize with strangers if you go with a couple you already know. That is, unless Barb and Frank are shameless matchmakers who are willing to lure charming bachelors to your table. Or your cart.

The best news about dating a man who likes to golf: He has his own friends and his own interests (okay, interest)—which means he won't be spending all his time hanging around your house in his bathrobe, hoping you'll entertain him.

Finally, don't worry about whether or not you're any good—nobody is.

Join a Motorcycle Gang

Over-forty men are drawn to Harley-Davidsons like flies to sugar cookies. Whether you join a local motorcycle "gang" (check your dealership for a group of enthusiasts in your area—some even host single-rider groups) or go it alone, motorcycle riding is another man-friendly pastime and a great way to get you out on the town. Just make sure you wear a helmet.

Marianne Williamson, Meet Wayne Dyer

If you're looking to meet someone as interested in self-growth as you are, attending lectures, conferences, and seminars by spiritual and self-development leaders can be a great place to start. Most of us get tear-our-hair-out frustrated by the frequent negativity of the male mind—and hanging out with a bunch of men who're actively seeking to live a more positive, meaningful, inspired life is a good place to start. Weekend conferences are best if you're hoping to meet other people, because they offer more chances to socialize than day-long seminars provide. If the conference feels too pricey, contact the organization or speaker and see if there's a way you can work at the event in exchange for free admission.

Yes, the crowd will be 70 percent women, but the men will be good ones.

Letters to Lisa ♥♥♥♥♥♥♥♥

Lisa,

I met a guy on a very popular Internet dating site. We met after a few emails, IMs, and phone conversations. He was very taken with me and pursued me with a vengeance. He did all of the right things—calling me, emailing me, making dates ahead of time, etc. I did sleep with him within the first couple of weeks. It moved very fast. He said he'd never gotten so involved with anyone so quickly and was taken by surprise by his feelings. Within a very short period of time, he said he loved me (two to three weeks after we met).

After dating about a month and a half, we took a weekend trip to my brother's beach house, where we had a glorious time together. While we were there, I told him I loved him, and he was caught off guard. It was a very awkward moment. Later that week, after the trip, he told me he was upset that I'd said that and that I had always been "ahead of him in the relationship." We talked through that, and things seemed okay.

But soon after, I could tell something wasn't right. He was still calling, making dates, and the usual, but I had that "pit" in my stomach telling me that he just wasn't as into it as much as he had appeared.

So, after a few weeks of feeling uneasy, I started to wonder if he was moving in another direction. I tried to call him; he didn't answer his phone. I checked the dating site, and sure enough, he had put his profile back on as active. We had made an agreement (his choice and suggestion) not to be visible and active, since we were dating each other exclusively.

So I pulled a "Glenn Close" (which I've never done in my life) and drove to his house. He answered the door, surprised that I showed up unannounced, and I asked him what was going on. I told him I saw his profile and wanted to know why he had broken that agreement. He said he was just on there "fooling around." He got angry at me for coming to his house, and of course, I was angry and upset to know he was seeking out other women.

We didn't speak for two days. He then sent an email that he missed me very much. We saw each other the next night, and again, everything was pleasant. But two nights later, he called and asked if he could come over and talk. He basically said his feelings weren't the same for me as they had been. He said he really cared for me and wanted to keep seeing me and being "friends." I told him I didn't know how to do that, since we'd begun dating under the guise of what I thought was intimacy and working into a possible relationship. I told him what I needed was to not see him.

We haven't spoken since. I've been going through the usual confusion and hurt and pain of it and wondering what was real and what was imagined. I've been divorced for many years and dated on and off during that time. I'm feeling sorry for myself that I trusted a man who seemed to have good intentions toward me, only to find out that maybe he never was really into me at all.

I know I'll get over him. But I'm having a hard time, because I thought that this guy was really into me and that I was doing it right this time. And it ended in complete disappointment.

Lost in Love

Dear Lost,

First off, this was not entirely your fault. In fact, it wasn't even mostly your fault. This guy pushes the relationship, tells you he loves you, and then freaks out when you return the sentiment a month later? Give me a break. He wants you to agree to take down your profiles, and then he puts his back up? And miraculously, all of this is your fault? I don't think so.

There are three things I want you to take away from this: First, don't sleep with a guy so early; otherwise you won't be able to clearly evaluate the relationship. Second, this guy is a one-off. It wasn't you; it was him. Third, no more Glenn Close. In this case, you were right to trust your intuition, but a surprise attack is rarely a good plan.

Hang in there, girl. The next one will be better.

Best,

Lisa

Romance and Power Tools

Most cities have some type of philanthropic singles organizations, and whether a group attracts young singles or mature singles depends on the city and the group. (Check out Senior Corps, www.seniorcorps.org, for volunteer groups for senior singles.)

The best part of meeting people through volunteer work? You help make the world a better place and meet a lot of like-minded eligibles. (Besides, helping others gives you good dating karma.) If there are no volunteer groups in your area catering specifically to singles, check out Habitat for Humanity, www.habitat.org. It's a great way to meet people of all ages, and you get to spend the day in the sunshine using power tools. What could be better?

Get Lucky in Vegas

Hit someplace cheap and sunny (Las Vegas or Mexico spring to mind). That fabulous combination of sand, salt water, and margaritas can be the perfect recipe for love. Or take your chance on the Robert Redford clone at the blackjack table. Go with as many same-sex friends as you can squeeze comfortably into a hotel room, and have the time of your life. And unlike trolling the bars, which can leave you feeling creepy and desperate, a vacation with your friends is fun and empowering. (Whether you meet someone or not.)

Too Tired or Busy To Date?

The other day I met a charming woman named Gina. She was in her late fifties and had been happily married to her husband for more than twenty years. He died unexpectedly, and Gina had been a widow for almost ten years.

"I'd like to get married again," she told me. "I miss having someone around to take care of, to love." And then she asked, "Can you find me a husband?"

I laughed with her and began to suggest some places she might go to meet some interesting men.

"Oh no," she said, "I'm too busy. I don't like to go out and meet people. I just like to stay home; I like to read; I don't really like to be around people." I suggested online dating, which she could do from the comfort of her own living room, and she told me she didn't trust computers. I suggested that because she loves reading, she might consider joining a book club or helping out at the library, but she said she couldn't be bothered. The more suggestions I made, the more excuses she offered. And as we talked, I realized that while she truly missed her husband and wanted the companionship she had in her marriage, she didn't really want to be back out in the world. She said she wanted a husband, but she was unable or unwilling to make space in her life to find one.

She was a sweet but complicated bundle of too busy, too afraid, couldn't be bothered, and didn't want to try. I realized that she was just hoping for a replacement guy to fill the dent in the mattress her husband had left. And pretty much any man who showed up at her house in his striped pajamas at 9:30 on a Thursday night could have the job.

"Can't you just send one to my house?" she'd asked.

I think she just didn't have the heart or the energy to open herself up to new people. When I suggested to her that her actions weren't really the actions of a woman looking to share her life with another person, she agreed and said that she didn't really want a husband. She wanted her husband back, the man who had passed away ten years before.

Just because you miss your husband doesn't mean you should go out and find another one.

The fact is, love usually doesn't show up unless you make a little room for it in your heart and your life. If you find yourself making excuses for why you can't go out or why trying to meet new people in a new way will never work, you're probably not ready yet.

And that's okay. Just because your Aunt Mildred or your best friend Christine thinks you should be back in the saddle by next Thursday, it doesn't mean you should.

You'll know when you're ready to find someone to love— because you won't be too afraid or busy to look.

Charity Benefits

Charity dinners do attract a moneyed crowd, but the best way to meet people will actually get you in for free. (Hey, there's no reason to put your nest egg in jeopardy just to have a fancy night out on the town. And be careful when you get there—one wild night with an auction paddle could have you eating cat food in your eighties.)

The secret to attending all the biggest charity benefits in your city? Volunteer! Volunteers generally eat for free, and you can go out on the town for as many nights as your closet will allow. Charities are always looking for warm bodies to help with auction items, take tickets, set up, and do other odd jobs on the day of the event. The best job? Checking people in at the door—you'll get to meet every person who attends and better yet, you'll know if that sharp-dressed charmer has tickets for two. Plus, it won't be blatantly obvious that you're flirting up a storm, because it's your job to be charming and nice.

Somebody Else's Company Picnic

Pair up with another single pal and survey his or her company's assets. These events are social, and as an added bonus, you know everybody there is employed. Your insider buddy can act as your tour guide to help you avoid the guy who sticks paper clips up his nose or the woman with fifty-nine cats.

Parties Once-Removed: Six Degrees of Barbecue

You know how you always invite the same seventeen people to all of your parties? Bring some new blood to the old gang. With Parties Once-Removed, everybody you invite brings someone that nobody else in the group knows. Think of it as six degrees of separation, only backwards. Voila! You'll have a party full of brand-new people who already get along great with your closest friends.

Grown-Up Dating Fact

Thirty-six percent of daters in our survey said that liking the same types of movies was an important factor in whether or not they'd date someone.

Throw Parties. Lots of Parties.

This is a bit of a continuation of Six Degrees of Barbecue, but one of the best ways to meet more new people is to entertain a lot. Why? Because the more parties you throw, the more parties you're invited to, thanks to the Law of Reciprocal Invitations. And sure, it may be the same old crowd at your place, but your friends know lots of people you don't. Every time you meet someone new or interesting, male or female, invite them to your next bash. Before you know it, your mailbox will be stuffed with invitations, and you'll be the neighborhood's very own "It Girl."

Become a Matchmaker

Fixing up your compatible friends might not seem like a great way to meet people at first glance, but it actually works amazingly well. Why? Say you set up two of your friends, Sam and Kate. They go on a date (thanks to you); they flirt over linguine and fall madly in love. Then they want to find some way to thank you for their newfound happiness. How do they do it? By racking their brains to figure out if they know anyone who could make you as happy as you've made them. Before you know it, you've got a date with Sam's accountant, Bernard, and Kate's taxidermist's next-door neighbor, Warren.

Expand Your Mind and Your Social Life

Hit your local adult-education center, and expand your mind (and your dating repertoire) in ways you never dreamed possible. Whether you take Palm Reading for Beginning Psychics, Toilet-Paper Origami, or even 362 Ways to Cook Chicken, you'll not only meet lots of interesting new people, but you may possibly discover a new talent as well.

How to Talk to a Stranger

Okay, so now you're armed with this giant list of places to meet someone, and you're thinking to yourself, *Well, this is all just lovely, but I'm not exactly the type to saunter over and say, "Hey baby, what's your sign?"*

The fact is, it's impossible to meet new people if you don't talk to strangers. *And if you're only talking to people you meet in official dating settings, you're missing out on a whole lot of opportunities.*

The Grown-Up Bottom Line: If you're hoping to meet someone, you should be talking to at least five strangers a day.

Most people get a little itchy at the idea of approaching someone they don't know, and the best way to get comfortable is to start when the stakes are low. Don't wait to try out your stranger-chatting skills until the exact moment when the George Clooney look-alike is ten feet away. Start practicing now with any man or woman who happens to be in front of you at the grocery-store checkout line ("How is that frozen coconut shrimp? I've been meaning to try it."), at the car wash ("Now that's a beautiful car. What made you decide on the burnt-sienna color?"), your mechanic's garage, the dry cleaners, the dog groomer, and anywhere else you hang out on a regular basis. You'll find the more you talk to people, the easier it will become.

Step one: Smile.

Step two: Start talking.

The easiest and most effective ways to strike up a conversation are to give a compliment, ask a question, ask for advice, or comment on something you can both see.

It's nearly always a safe bet to compliment a woman on something she's wearing and a man on what he's doing (such as the way he just handled a situation). If a man holds the door, give your brightest smile and say something like, "Where did you learn such wonderful manners?"

Asking a question or requesting advice are surefire ways to spark a chat, because you're instantly engaging the other person, and common courtesy will usually guarantee at least one round of conversation ("Have you had good luck using those mesquite chips when you're grilling a steak?" "How long do you think we're supposed to stand on the corner holding these Vote Today signs?") It makes people feel good to be able to provide an answer, even if the question is a simple one. Be sure to avoid questions that have a yes or no answer—you want to start a conversation, not conduct an inquisition.

Finally, if you have a good sense of humor, it can be incredibly effective to crack a joke about something you both see—a shared experience. Whether it's the woman and her Yorkipoo wearing matching pink, sparkly bikinis or a skateboarding octogenarian, the world is your punch line.

Sea of Love

If you like to travel, take advantage of the many singles cruises and single vacation packages available these days. You can cruise to Alaska to see the glaciers, kick your heels up at a dude ranch, or cook your way through Tuscany—wherever you go, most tour packages offer lots of opportunities to meet new people.

In addition, many vacation packages and cruises are targeted to specific groups, such as Jewish or Christian singles, those over thirty-five, baby boomers, and even seniors. Be sure to ask the vacation coordinator what types of male-to-female ratios they generally attract; fifty-fifty is a rarity, but many vacations come close, and a few will have odds in your favor, with a higher ratio of men to women.

Many women I've met over the last several years encountered their future spouses on singles vacations—on cruises, hiking adventures, and culinary trips. Better still, most people have a great experience with their singles vacations, whether they spark a love connection or not.

Love Boat Notes

Both Carrie and Lori met their future husbands on singles cruises (SinglesCruise.com).

"I am really thankful and blessed that through SinglesCruise. com, I have met and made lifelong friendships with amazing people, including my soul mate," says Carrie, who met her future husband met on a cruise in 2004 and cemented the relationship in 2005. "We have spoken on the phone every day and have seen each other every eight to ten weeks, even though I live in Texas and he lives in England. He proposed during my family vacation in Key West, and we are now planning [our] wedding."

Carrie adds that what she liked best about meeting her fiancé on a singles cruise was the ease and comfort. "Since we were part of the same group, we were sort of already bonded.

Because we were on the ship for a limited amount of time, we tried to make the most of the time we had and focused on learning more about each other faster."

Another singles cruiser, Lori, said, "A singles cruise gives you the opportunity to meet other interesting people and create friendships from all over the world. I went on my first singles cruise in April 2005, not looking for that special someone but for fun and sun. I had such a great time and met so many new friends, some of whom I stay in touch with to this day. On my second singles cruise over Halloween 2005, I still wasn't looking for a serious relationship, but I ended up meeting my future husband."

Join the Club

From wood carving to reading to *Star Trek* to writing the Great American Novel, there are clubs for just about everything. You can find them listed in the local newspaper, posted at the library, or at online sites, like Meetup.com. Some groups have age requirements, others don't; but your best bet is to keep an open mind, and join others in doing things you love to do.

Holy Hotties!

If you are a religious person, the first place you should be looking for love is at your church. Join the singles group, or start one if your church doesn't have one already. Take every class your church offers (most of them are free); volunteer to be the greeter on Sunday; or join the new-membership committee (you'll get first dibs on any new prospects). And if your congregation's singles scene isn't what you're hoping for, consider joining a group sponsored by another church in your area.

Change the World, One Date at a Time

Our generation has the strongest change-the-world gene of any generation ever born, which is why so many are volunteering for political campaigns, charities, community votes, and grassroots organizations. Get involved at the national or local level with a cause you can respect. You'll not only meet lots of smart, civic-minded people, but you can be sure that most of them will share many of your world views. As an added bonus, the victory parties are always wild events.

It's Fun to Date at the YMCA

The men tend to steer clear of the classes and stick to the weights, so if you're a woman, you might consider working out on the machines. (You can always ask the charming gentleman next to you for help if you're not quite sure what you're doing, and besides, weight lifting is good for bone density!)

Go, Go, Tigers

The older you get, the more popular events at your alma mater become. If you're looking for love or just a night out on the town, make sure you don't skip your class reunion or the local tailgate for the big homecoming game. Be sure to join your alumni association, which will keep you alerted to local events and gatherings in your area. Many cities have local alumni chapters or groups that meet regularly to watch sporting events and socialize.

Old Flames: Should You Fan the Fire or Expect a Burnout?

Romance novels and Hollywood movies are filled with stories of couples who've reunited after thirty, forty, or even fifty years apart, the ones whose fairy-tale endings fuel the possibilities in our pasts. Often when we're in a love-life lull, whether we're in a relationship or alone, we start thinking about the ghosts of lovers past. We remember with fondness the one who got away—while jealous spats, lackluster sex, complete and utter incompatibility, and even chronic cheating are conveniently erased by the passing of time.

We imagine picking up where we left off, our memories buzzing with corsages, first kisses, and the happily-ever-after optimism of youth, easily forgetting that the thing that caused the original rift is probably still lurking just beneath the surface. But hope springs eternal.

Jane and Tim★ dated back in high school. He was madly in love; she was sixteen and popular. They broke up after he joined the Marines and left town. She was, he says, the great love of his life, and he has a tattoo on his arm to prove it. He was, by her estimation, a very nice boy. Some forty-five years later, he's a widower, and Jane is single again after a nearly thirty-year marriage. They connected once again online through a mutual friend from high school.

Tim would like to pick right back up where they left off more than forty years ago and has even suggested marriage. Jane is happy being single, and while she's fond of Tim and enjoys their late-night phone chats, she says, "I'm not going there."

Sometimes, circumstances—from family to obligations to career choices—get in the way of what might have been a successful relationship. In that case, a rekindling can work.

Dennis met Erika on a cruise twenty-one years ago. They dated on and off for five years, even though she was from St. Louis and he was from Boston. They both ended up in Phoenix, where they dated, but it didn't last. They were young and had different priorities. Both of them eventually married other people.

Dennis says, "Ironically, our families remained in contact even when Erika and I did not—my mother attended Erika's first wedding but didn't attend mine, because she didn't approve. At the time, she told Erika's mother, 'The only thing that would make this better is if my son was up there.'"

Both Erika and Dennis got divorced from their respective partners, and then four years ago, they reconnected. "Erika and I emailed each other, talked on the phone, and two weeks later, I made my first trip to Phoenix to visit her," says Dennis, who had moved back to Boston. "I knew the minute I saw her at the airport that we were going to be together for good this time." (She says she didn't know until his second visit.) They are now married and have a child.

The Internet has made it exceedingly easy to search out old friends and loves. A few minutes with your favorite search engine and you can find out that your ex beau has his own law firm or won Teacher of the Year. In a recent Classmates.com poll, 40 percent of respondents had used the Internet to look up or reconnect with an old boyfriend or girlfriend, and 78 percent reflected on their first love or high-school sweetheart when thinking about their love life.

Maybe you're bored. Maybe you're lonely. Maybe your love life sucks. Maybe you'd like to feel the same way you did in high school, swaying to the music at the homecoming dance, heart pounding in anticipation of what the night might bring. Maybe you'd like a do-over, a chance to replay a time in your life when you made mistakes.

When you attempt to reconnect with an old flame, both of you have expectations from the first relationship—and it's likely that one or both of you will end up being disappointed.

In most cases, you can't go home again. There was a reason you broke up the first time, and more than likely it will still be there on the second, or the twenty-ninth, go-around. You've been living your life; he's been living his; and neither of you are the same person you were five or ten or twenty years ago. Sometimes that is a problem—you're hoping to be with someone who doesn't exist anymore.

Other times, however, your shared experiences and time apart will help you to form a stronger bond. Proceed with caution, and see where your situation stacks up.

When Rekindling Works

- You were too young when you first met.

- Your families interrupted the relationship or kept you apart.

- You broke up to pursue your dreams.

When Rekindling Fizzles

You broke up because of . . .

- Cheating

- Jealousy

- Chronic fighting

Act Like You Want It

Try out for your local theater productions—they're a great way to meet new people if you're creatively inclined. And if you're not interested in being the star of the show, most productions can use a hand with scenery, stage effects, or costumes.

Florida

Trust me. I live here. The entire state is just teeming with hotties over forty.

Narrow Your Search

Last but not least, online dating and speed dating can also be great ways to meet lots of new people, but both can be loaded with disaster if you don't know what you're doing—we'll cover tips for doing both successfully in Chapters 6 and 7.

What's most important to remember is that you'll meet more compatible men by putting a magnifying glass on who *you* are and what you're looking for. If you're seeking a religious mate, don't hang out at the grocery store, hoping to hook up with a spiritual man in the melon section—start looking at your church. If you're hoping for a date who loves reading as much as you do, start your search at a book club or your local library. Think about what you really love, whether it's bird watching, snorkeling, or breeding ferrets for show, and expand that area of your life. Take more classes; join more clubs. Expand your circle of acquaintances in that particular area of your existence so you'll have a better chance of meeting someone who either shares your passion, or at least respects it.

Most of all, remember that you've earned a little fun, and everybody deserves a second (or third or, okay, forty-seventh) chance at love.

Now all you have to do is go out and get it.

Chapter 4
Why Older Women Are (Finally) Dating Younger Men

Attack of the Cougars

Boy toy. Man candy. Himbo.

A few years ago, such words didn't even exist. Now they're practically on the short list for inclusion in *Webster's*.

It seems the May–December romance has developed a whole new twist. Instead of being doomed to spinsterhood or senior sex after the ripe old age of forty, mature women are chucking the shackles of propriety and hooking up with younger guys just for the fun of it. And (*gasp*) they're finding out what rich guys, politicians, and men knee-deep in a midlife crisis have known all along. Dating somebody younger is fun. Lots of fun.

Why the recent trend? Two reasons. First, the "older women" of today are not your grandma's grandmas. We take care of ourselves, we're working out, and we're confident and established in our careers. In other words, we've got what younger women have, and then some.

The second reason? The "woman shortage" building up over the last several years has a lot of men considering options they hadn't before.

Grown-Up Dating Fact

By the year 2010, there will be 1 million extra men in the 25–44 age range. Those bachelors in the prime of their lives won't just sit around crying in their soup about the lack of available women—they'll be pursuing women over forty.

Source: U.S. Census Bureau

For many women, the decision to date younger men stems from a desire for a relationship with fewer complications and more sex. Younger men have less baggage, fewer ex-wives, and frankly, they don't have the saggy, wrinkly butts of their middle-aged counterparts.

With Demi Moore (Ashton Kutcher) and Madonna (Guy Ritchie) leading the way and film and magazines jumping right on board, being a "cougar" (a term first used in 1999 to indicate an older woman dating a younger man) is practically a status symbol.

But what's in it for the guys?

As we've discussed, mature women have a lot to offer. You're more experienced, confident, independent, and self-sufficient, which is a huge turn-on for many men. You also don't have as much insecurity about your body, and sometimes you're just looking for sex without the strings.

In guy world, that's a slam dunk.

Some women, like my friend Lisa Earle McLeod (www.forget-perfect.com), aren't sure the benefits outshine the downside: "It must start when you're drunk. The attention of a younger man is flattering, but who wants to hold in her stomach for the next thirty years?"

She's joking, of course, but she brings up a valid point. There is a downside.

Some women find they're still uncomfortable with the idea of dating "down," whether it's someone younger, less–educated, or less established in his career. Many women don't feel comfortable shucking the classic ideals of the taller, richer, older, more successful mate. Others who have tried dating younger men found the experience fun, but felt that, ultimately, the emotional connection they were seeking could only be found with someone their own age. And as fabulous as it may be to *be with* a hot young thing, it's sometimes far better to *be* the hot young thing yourself.

Lisa cracks, "I want to be the cute, young hottie in the relationship. Of course, that means if my current husband dumps me, I'm going to have to start cruising nursing homes at cocktail time."

As for long-term relationships, Lisa sums it up like this: "Date a younger guy but marry an older one. Somebody is going to get old and fat first, and it's not going to be me."

Enough said.

7 Secrets of the Cougars: Why Younger Men Love Them

- Cougars are comfortable holding the power in the relationship.

- Cougars are secure with their looks and their bodies, even if they're not perfect.

- Cougars tend to have a wide variety of interests, which makes an age gap less significant (and makes it easier to meet younger men).

- Cougars usually are not concerned with what others think of them.

- Cougars are generally not looking for a provider or someone to have a family with—they're self-sufficient.

- Cougars are generally not tied down with traditional roles.

- Cougars are in it for fun or sex.

Being a Cougar Is Not for Everyone

If you're looking for a committed relationship, dating a younger man may not be the way to go. Sure, there are lots of examples of May–December couples who live happily every after, but one of the great appeals on both sides of the older woman–younger man dynamic is that the issue of commitment isn't much of an issue. Usually, neither side wants a long-term attachment. Which means if you find yourself attached in the relationship (and sex makes women feel more bonded), you may be in for heartbreak.

The Cougar Hunters

Many women are offended by the term "cougar," because it seems like such a predatory word, but an interesting side effect of the cougar phenomenon is the cougar hunters: young men in their early twenties and thirties who go out to bars and other popular haunts in search of cougars. There is a dress code among these men—the artfully tousled hair, the status jeans paired with a blazer. The key is to look young and movie-star (or, more accurately, soap-star) confident without looking like someone's teenage son. Most of the hunters are looking for sex, hoping for a side of gifts or money. It is the cougar hunters who will buy the drinks at the bar, but the cougars will be paying for the gym memberships, the vacations, and sometimes the rent. Now who's being stalked?

Grown-Up Dating Fact

According to a recent study by *AARP the Magazine,* 34 percent of women over forty are dating younger men.

Letters to Lisa

Dear Lisa,

My problem is with my boyfriend of six months. In the beginning, he was so romantic. Now, EVERY SINGLE TIME he sets a date for us to go out somewhere, he is at least forty-five minutes late.

The first few times it happened, I waited at home until he called an hour later with an excuse, asking if we were still on. I would tell him I was upset, but I would still go (teaching him that I would put up with it). One time, we were supposed to go to a jazz club, and he said he would be at my apartment at 8:30. Time passed . . . and passed . . . and before

I knew it, I had fallen asleep on my couch waiting for him, but he never showed up. He called the next day and said that he had run into some of his friends who were heading out for a night on the town, and he didn't call because he knew I would be mad. He figured that by calling the next day, I would have time to cool off.

I've brought this to his attention several times and he says he understands, yet he continues to do it. Why could this be happening?

Tired of Mr. Tardy

Dear Tired,

People can only treat us as badly as we allow them to treat us.

It's time to take serious action. The next time you have a date with this guy, wait no more than twenty minutes, and then without any warning whatsoever to him, leave your house and go out with some friends. When he calls later to find out why you weren't waiting around, tell Mr. Tardy that you think he's a fabulous guy and you enjoy your time together, but you refuse to waste your time hanging around on the couch, watching bad TV and waiting for a guy who may or may not show up. Then tell him that from now on, you will wait no more than fifteen minutes for him to show up. Then, stick to your guns (or in this case, your clock). If he's late, leave. Date cancelled. If he can't get his act together, he's just not worth your time.

Best,

Lisa

Chapter 5

How to Date Like a Grown-Up

Daters, Meet Reality

Probably the most important lesson in dating like a grown-up is in facing reality. Some things work; some things don't.

The guidelines you'll find in this chapter tend to skew on the traditional side (turns out Mom was right all along!), and there's a reason for that: it's what works best.

There are two things you should know about me: I consider myself to be a feminist, and I am extremely practical. Which means that even though I *can* open my own door and pay for my own dinner, I let the guy do it. Why? It makes him feel like a man. Better still, it makes him *act* like a man.

Men and women are biologically compelled to behave in certain ways, and we can either fight our natural instincts or work with them. I can tell you from experience and years of research that everybody is a lot happier when we let nature take its course.

The good news is that modern men have spent the last forty years with working wives, working mothers, and competent women at the office. The fact that you allow him to pull out your chair or buy you a steak is certainly not going to give him the mistaken impression that you are incapable of doing it yourself. In fact, he will find you stronger when you are secure enough to embrace your femininity.

Men are biologically programmed to pursue women and prove their worth to potential partners by exhibiting their status and desirability as a mate. How does he do that? By giving you an indication of his ability as a provider, which boils down to his career or social position and his financial status. It's been that way since Ugg the Caveman pursued the lovely cavewoman next door, and it hasn't changed in thousands of years. When you grab the check or chase him down like prey, you are short-circuiting his ability to show you he's a worthwhile mate.

Besides being easier on everybody, there is another benefit to letting the guy take the lead: If you pursue him, he may accept a date with you because he doesn't want to hurt your feelings or because he thinks he may have just lucked into some easy action. Online dating has muddled things even further (for more on how these rules apply to online dating, see Chapter 7), but here's the bottom line: If you allow him to pursue you, he'll usually only expend the effort do so because he finds you genuinely appealing. Which means you won't be wasting your time with someone who's not actually interested in you. The harder he has to work to get you to date him, the more he values the relationship.

Make him work for it. Here's how to do that.

Never Ask a Man for a Date. Ever.

I know I'm harping on it, but men need to be men, and you can either work with that little bit of information or spend the rest of your life working against it. Let the guy do the asking.

The very same brain cells that make him need to be the instigator in the relationship are also the ones that compel him to give you his coat when it gets chilly outside, step in front of you if you ever meet up with a mugger in a dark alley, or kill the really big, nasty flying bug in your bathroom. Trust me, these are good brain cells.

I can hear you now: "What if the man is just terribly shy and would never ask me out if I didn't make the first move?" (It's a question I get on a regular basis.)

The answer is if he doesn't ask you out, he doesn't really want to date you. I know this may be a shocker, but any man, no matter how shy, will muster the courage if he truly wants to ask you for a date. (It might take him a while, but it will happen eventually.)

Here's what happens in the man's brain when you ask him on a date: He either thinks you're sort of desperate or wonders what's wrong with you. After all, if you're so great, why isn't somebody else dating you? He may even go out with you a few times, but trust me, the relationship will be doomed. He will never truly value you because of this simple fact: *he didn't have to work hard to get you.*

As we all know, anything worth having is worth working for.

Who Should Pay?

"I used to say the woman, and then I'd say the couple; and now I think a guy should step up and just be a gentleman and pay for the damn thing."
—From the Grown-Up Dating Survey

Call me old-fashioned (you won't be the first), but I think the man should pay. What's more is that nearly all of the thousands of men I've interviewed over the years think they should pay, too. Here's how the grown-up dater sees it: The man should ask you for the date; he should plan the date; and of course, as your host, he should always pay for the dates.

First, it's traditional, and most men are pretty traditional at heart. Second, a man who truly wants to spend time with you will be more than happy to pick up the check. He will, in fact, value you more if he is doing most of the legwork for the two of you to be together. If he's investing his time, money, and emotion in you, he won't just hold you in greater esteem; he'll also continue to work even harder to keep you. Men know that nothing of value comes easily or cheaply. Your every action shows your dates that you are worth being with—including letting him pay for dinner. Yes, I know that you can afford to pay half. More than likely, your date knows that, too. And it is a lovely gesture when you politely offer to pick up the check.

But most men tell me they really *prefer* to pay for dates. Men find it a little embarrassing and emasculating when the waiter presents the bill, usually to him, and his date snatches it up and whips out the old MasterCard.

Remember, deciding who picks up the tab is not about *what he thinks of you;* it's about *what you think of him.*

The Dating Rotation

Women tend to be serial monogamists. We date one man at a time, see how the guy pans out, and go back out and do it all over again when the relationship doesn't work.

Men, on the other hand, date a number of women at the same time until they meet one they'd like to pursue a relationship with. This is a much smarter strategy.

This is not coincidentally why women will work harder to keep a so-so relationship from falling apart—we know if we let it go, we'll have to start back at square one.

Here's how the rotation works: At all times you are *not* in an exclusive relationship, you should date (rotate) three men—the pair and the spare. In the event that you have a full rotation (are dating three men) and someone new you would like to date asks you out, you simply drop your least favorite guy from the group and mix in the new one.

Why would you do that? The reasons for dating three men at a time instead of one are simple.

- First, rotation takes your mind off any one man. You won't obsess over whether or not a man is going to ask you out on Saturday night, because if he doesn't, one of the other two will. Sure, men can smell desperation a mile away, but the opposite is true as well. When they have competition, at some level, they sense it. And men always want you a lot more when they're not exactly sure how many players are in the game.

- Second, dating three men at a time keeps your schedule pretty full. Not only will you have as many dates as you can handle, but you won't ever have to *play* hard to get—because you'll actually *be* hard to get. Plus, having so many men competing for your time is spectacular for your self-esteem. Every guy on your rotation will be making himself nutty wondering what you're doing with

the time you're not available to go out with him and trying to figure out how he can have you all for himself.

- Third, you get to date three different guys at a time, without worrying if one of them is "the one." Your needs for
sex, a tennis partner, or someone who "gets" abstract art
will be easily met by your "frankendate" of three men,
without you feeling like you need to hold out for the
perfect guy or mold one into what you truly want.

- So what happens when one of the guys wants a promotion
to "the" guy? If one of your men asks to date you exclusively and you'd like to take the relationship in that direction,
gently let your other suitors know that you've met someone
else and you want to see where the relationship goes. If you
do it right, the bachelors you've released will always think
of you as "the one who got away."

- You may wonder, *why date three men and not two or four?*
As far as I'm concerned, three is the magic number. (Two
doesn't keep you busy enough or offer enough variety,
and four, well, that feels less like dating and more like
crowd control.) An ambitious woman may be able to successfully rotate four men, but eventually we all have to
dedicate a little time to important tasks like work, REM
sleep, and leg waxing.

One final note: Do not have sex while you are rotating men.
You are a fun, desirable, interesting woman. You are not a
tramp. Besides, you're far more likely to get hurt feelings if sex
is involved.

Letters to Lisa

Dear Lisa,

What are your thoughts on dating more than one person at a time? I've been dating online for a few months with no luck, and last week I met two really nice gentlemen online and hit it off with both of them. I met each of them for dinner and would like to see where things go. It feels too early to make a decision about either one, but I don't want to be dishonest either. Should I continue to date them both? And if I do, should I tell them about each other?

When It Rains, It Pours

Dear Rains,

First of all, clearly you're a sweet, sensitive woman who doesn't want to hurt anyone's feelings. There are too few people like you in the world. That said, there's nothing wrong with dating two gentlemen casually. The key is to keep things honest, and don't enter into an exclusive relationship if you want to keep playing the field. You have two choices here, as I see it. You can take a wait-and-see approach with both men and 'fess up if one of them asks about any other roosters lurking around in your life. Or you can decide which of these two guys you like the most, drop the other one, and pursue an exclusive relationship with the man you like. Either way, you have to do what's comfortable for you.

Best,

Lisa

The Two-Day Rule

Never accept a date unless the man has asked you out at least forty-eight hours in advance. This means a man should call you no later than Wednesday for a Friday night date. The two-day rule applies to weekdays as well, although it's a good policy to use a three-days-in-advance notice for Saturday night dates. This is important for several reasons.

First, it lets the guy know right away that you are not sitting around in your pajamas waiting for him to call. You have a busy, active life, after all, and your time is in demand. This may initially come as a shock to him, but when he realizes you're not waiting for him to ask you out, you'll be more appealing to him than ever. You might be concerned that a man will not ask you out again if you turn down a date. Amazingly, just the opposite is true. Instead of assuming you don't like him, he'll likely be more persistent and ask you out next time with more notice. He'll probably spend a little time wondering where you are and what you're doing without him. This stokes the competitive part of his brain a little, and then he starts thinking, *if you're so popular, there must be something* really *fabulous about you.* He will also get his first (and probably not last) taste of the fact that you are quite a busy woman and if he wants to spend time with you, he'll have to plan ahead. Some men do this automatically; others need to be guided to more gentlemanly behavior.

Second, the two-day rule protects you from sitting around all weekend, waiting for the phone to ring. If he hasn't called by Wednesday or Thursday, you know you'll need to make other plans for Saturday night and stick to them. Go to dinner with any similarly situated girlfriends, book a pedicure, or go see a movie or an art exhibit with a co-worker. Whatever you do, make unbreakable plans with someone else. (This will keep you from making any exceptions in a moment of lust or desperation.) And when an uninitiated man calls for a last-minute date night, you can kindly and honestly tell him that you would have liked to go out with him, but you already have plans.

The last thing you need is to be hanging around your living room watching some cheeseball TV program and wishing you had something to do. On the flip side, the man you're dating, having been turned down for asking you out with not enough notice, will spend his time thinking about you. Not such a bad deal, eh?

Remember, you only want to date a guy who really *wants* to spend time with you, who *thinks* about spending time with you, and who *respects* you enough to treat you as though you have a life that is quite full with or without him. You are not a booty call or a last resort. You're a fabulous woman in high demand.

Don't Call Them—They'll Call You

Never call a man. Sure, you may have heard this one before. There's a reason for that. It's because *you should never call a man.*

Women are multitaskers; men are single-taskers.

We can talk on the phone, do our taxes, touch up our roots, and julienne potatoes, all at the same time. Men can't.

If you call him, he'll likely be in the middle of something else, and he'll seem distracted. Then you'll start wondering, *Is everything okay? Why does he seem so distant? Why does he seem so weird?*

And then you ask him, *Is everything okay?* And he says yes, but you don't believe him; and then you get into a forty-five-minute conversation about whether everything is or isn't okay (and by the time the conversation ends, it isn't). You hang up the phone feeling confused and insecure. He hangs up wondering what the hell just happened.

All because you called him and caught him in the middle of his nose-hair clipping ritual. Or a crossword puzzle. Or watching Ultimate Fighting Championship.

Men focus on one thing at a time. Which means if you call him—unless you happen to catch him at the exact moment when he was about to call you—he is thinking about something else or doing something else, and you'll feel as though you've interrupted him.

Let him call you.

In order for a man to be truly intrigued by you, he must do the pursuing. He must be the one thinking of you, thinking of a good reason to call you, planning what to say, and wondering if *you* really want to talk to *him*. Best of all, every time you talk on the phone, it will be because *he wants to talk to you*. You'll never catch him at a bad time, so you'll always have his full attention and desire.

Many women have a hard time with this idea; maybe it feels like a loss of control. What's important to remember is that you're going to have a better connection, with a more personal conversation, if you let him do the calling.

Now, you might be thinking of all sorts of reasons why it should be okay to call a man. What if he calls you first? What if he tried to call during the three seconds when you were ordering Chinese takeout, and he got a busy signal? What if he lost your phone number? What if your phone is broken? Here's the answer: *Never call a man.*

If he really wants to talk to you, he'll call back. If he loses your phone number and really wants to talk to you, he'll track you down.

You may think that a man will assume you don't like him if you never call him back. That's incredibly logical, but it just isn't true. Something as ambiguous as not returning calls is not seen as a rejection to most men. (Because, after all, you haven't actually told him no.) Men, if they notice at all, will see this as a challenge.

And every guy loves a challenge.

Never Say It First

When it comes to saying "I love you," it is crucial to let the man take the leap. Remember, men need to feel that they are leading the relationship; otherwise they start dragging their feet. Guys want to be with a woman who makes them feel like a man.

You may want to hear "I love you" a lot sooner than he says it, but trust me, if he feels it, he'll say it eventually. (And if he doesn't feel it, confessing your deepest emotions certainly isn't going to bring him around.)

Some guys are a little shy about the "L" word. I once heard somewhere that a man knows whether or not he is in love after just a few dates, while it takes a woman around a dozen dates before she starts feeling that way. After interviewing hundreds of men and women about this topic, the numbers hold up. Most men and women I spoke with felt that timeline was right on the money. Try to keep this in mind when things seem like they're going well, and you start wondering when he's going to say those three little words. By the time you've started to feel it, he may have been feeling it for a while, and the big moment is likely imminent. Just be patient. You are, after all, the most secure, amazing women he's ever met, right? Of course he'll fall madly in love with you! Just be sure you let him say it first.

Speaking of things you shouldn't say to a man, don't use the word "marriage" or "wedding," even in passing. It freaks them out.

> **"Most women have lost the art of subtly moving aside so that a guy can hold the door open for them. It's hard to be a gentleman when your date just barrels through the door without giving you a chance."**
> **—Mark, TV Producer**

Letters to Lisa　

Dear Lisa,

I met a guy who is really nice, but my girlfriends say I am too eager for my own good. I return his calls immediately; I talk about him a lot; and I'm making his life as a doctor the center of my life. I read your book and I'm not sure what to do. Am I too eager? Or am I just afraid of letting another good catch slip away?

Very Afraid

Dear Afraid,

I'm afraid for you, darling.

Are you too eager? Yes. How is it that his profession is the center of your life?

Don't worry about letting this good catch slip through your fingers— if you keep this up, you'll drive him away. I'm assuming when you said you'd read my book that you really meant that you were using it for a doorstop. Why? Because 1) if you had read it you'd know that doctor-worshipping is strictly prohibited, or 2) if you read it but thought the book was full of bad advice, you likely wouldn't be writing to me now, right? I'm sure you're an amazing woman, but let me clear a few things up for you. In any relationship, both people need to have their own lives. It never works if one person has a life, and the other person thinks they'll just live off that like some kind of human leech. You need your own friends, your own hobbies, and your own fabulous job.

You may have found a good catch, but he's found a groupie.

How about putting a little of that energy you're using on the doc to better use? Spend a little of that effort figuring out who you want to be and how you can be as impressed with your own accomplishments as you are with his.

Best,

Lisa

Should You Google Your Dates?

Ask any woman if she googles her dates, and the answer is frequently yes. (Or, "Why—what have you heard?") Thanks to the magic of Google, you can learn that your date-to-be was winner of the National Peanut-Brittle-Eating Competition, was recently married in a lovely ceremony at the Kiwanis Club, or is currently serving five to ten for impersonating a real-estate agent.

To some, googling your date feels like a natural extension to online dating. After all, the technology is there, so why not use it? To others, googling seems like an invasion of the privacy of a stranger. It's like being left alone in a guy's apartment for the first time: Should you sit on the couch, innocently flipping through the pages of *In Style* and awaiting his return? Or should you use the 13.6 minutes he'll be gone on a pizza run to rummage through the shoebox on the high shelf in his closet, check his nightstand drawers for evidence, and listen to the saved messages on his answering machine?

As one online dater put it, "No!!!! Don't google dates! I was dating a divorced guy I met online, and when I googled him, I found an interview with his ex-wife. I had her picture staring at me, found out their wedding date and details of their honeymoon, etc. I felt like I had just committed a major invasion of privacy. How was I supposed to react when it got to the point that this man was going to confide those details to me?"

But other daters feel it's a matter of safety. A single mother of two met a man online who turned out to be a con artist. He forged checks, cleaned out her bank account, and eventually forced her into foreclosure. She warns, "Is it okay to check out dates? I say it is critical!"

As women, we must do everything we can to keep ourselves safe. Among the tools of curious and safety-conscious daters is the reverse phone-number lookup offered by Google (just type a phone number into the search box to get the corresponding name and address listed in the phone book—which can serve as a red flag if a woman's name comes up), as well as a plethora of online detectives who, for a small fee, can search out everything from marriages to diplomas to bankruptcies to DUIs.

The truth is, there is a lot of information available. And there's a fine line between keeping yourself safe (good), satisfying your curiosity (not *so* bad), and invading someone's privacy (cue "stalker" music).

And while I'm not in favor of snooping through someone's underwear drawer while he runs down to the convenience store, I do think googling is a pretty good idea. After all, any information you find on Google is probably a matter of public record anyway. It's not as though you're breaking into the FBI mainframe to view secret files. Where googling can help is to bring up any red flags: Maybe your new guy has been blogging a turkey-baster manifesto. Maybe that charming man has a thirty-eight-page rap sheet. Maybe that promising guy, who says he's a partner at a big downtown law firm, doesn't show up on the firm website—maybe it's because he's new; maybe it's because he works in the mailroom.

Either way, it's smarter to look for love with your heart *and* your eyes wide open.

Not Another Movie Date! Six Rambunctious Date Ideas to Get You Out of the Theater

As I've mentioned already, I'm all for letting the gentleman plan and host your dates. But occasionally, you may be asked to contribute some ideas, so it might be fun to get out of the rut of the same ol,' same ol.'

While movies are great, they're frequently a horrible date. Why? No talking and, other than what's on the screen, no imagination. Frankly, in the great running history of romance we all have in our heads, another action flick with a side of spaghetti doesn't even register a blip. So whether you're on your first date or your forty-first, pass on the popcorn. Just check out the ideas below for six dates that will get your heart pounding in more ways than one.

Roller-Skating at a Roller-Skating Rink Date

Take your date back to the fifth grade—to a world where

glittering disco balls, neon shoelaces, and doing the Y.M.C.A are still cool. Sure, neither one of you will be able to skate backwards, and first-graders hopped up on birthday cake will probably leave you in the dust, but at least you'll know you're hooked up when they turn down the lights for the "couples skate."

So geek, it's chic.

Habitat for Humanity Date

You're not just a great date; you're a great human being! Nothing brings people close together like doing something for others. You'll be tired; you'll be proud; and you'll be an ace with a circular saw. For a project near you, check out www.habitat.org. The atmosphere is great; you can pack your own picnic; and you'll both have the chance to show off your better side. Whether you help out for a single Saturday or dedicate yourself for a lifetime, it will be a date neither one of you will ever forget.

Ballroom Dancing Date

With the popularity of crooners on the rise, it only makes sense that ballroom dancing would be making a comeback in a huge way. It's romantic, it's fun, and most girls adore a guy who can really twirl them around on the dance floor.

Not only that, it's a great way to get close (and get your heart pounding) in a nonthreatening way. There's nothing that makes a woman swoon like a guy who can cut a rug. Lots of studios have beginner nights and one-time lessons; for a dance studio near you, check out DanceNet (www.havetodance.com), which offers links and info on studios in the United States and Canada.

The Flying Wallinskis Date

There are a bunch of new "experience" sites cropping up online, offering everything from flying-trapeze lessons, where you learn to "fly" like circus performers, to NASCAR driving, where you can actually do a couple laps in a real NASCAR race car, to cave exploring, where you, well, explore caves. What's surprising is that many of the options are quite affordable (as in, under $50). Check out Wallbounce (www.wallbounce.com), Great American Days (www.greatamericandays.com), and Total Experience (www.totalexperience.ca) for an adventure near you. Offerings vary by region and season, so you never know what thrills may lie in your own backyard.

Horseback Riding

Pack a picnic lunch and take advantage of a chance to slow down and enjoy the ride. Most riding stables will let you rent a horse for an hour or a half day. We ladies love cowboys. Even if it's temporary.

Book-Signing Date

It's different. It's interesting. And it's going on at a bookstore near you. And as long as you don't pick a title like *Twenty-Five Years of Cute Cats* or *Encyclopedia of Mold and Spores,* your date will think you're smart, and you'll have something to talk about when you get coffee afterward. Most authors do book signings, but even the famous ones hardly ever draw more than a few people (except that damned dog Mr. Winkle—his book signings usually have crowd-control personnel worthy of visiting royalty and a line of screaming fans around the block). Get your books signed (as long as you're there, you might as well get a couple— personalized books make great holiday gifts); enjoy the discussion and the free coffee; and spend some time chatting with the author. You'll have a souvenir from your date, and you might just start your own book club for two.

No Date Is Ever Wasted

My friend Tina is a seriously successful online dater. I mean six-dates-in-five-days kind of successful. Now, granted, she has a lot going for her: she's smart; she's beer-shooting-out-your-nose funny; and she has a major career in advertising. She's also got a J. Lo booty and a smile so fabulous, it puts Julia Roberts to shame. It's practically made for HDTV.

Ladies, before you start sighing and, you know, vomiting, you should know this: Tina is not a size-two, Marcia-Brady-haired, Junior-League blonde. She's a normal woman. What makes her so appealing is that she practically oozes confidence and has this utterly compelling interest in other people: who they are, what they do and why they like it, what makes them jump up and down. Where most people put forth a huge amount of effort just trying to *be interesting,* Tina immediately connects with people because she is effortlessly *interested.*

Having known her for nearly fifteen years, I'm most amazed by Tina's unique ability to convert the guys she meets online who aren't exactly boyfriend material to friends. And business contacts. And matchmakers for her. As in, no opportunity wasted. When most online daters have a date with no sparks, they never talk to the person again (even if they're nice) and just head back to the keyboard. Tina realizes, however, that even if it's not a romantic match, the two of them have something (probably a lot of somethings) in common, and she maintains the relationship— even as just a social contact.

Not a perfect match? Tina says, "Who knows? You may have just found your new podiatrist. Your new taxidermist. Or your new brother-in-law."

Because Tina works in advertising, she is compelled by the

industry to find a new job every couple of years. Her last job was as the vice president of new business at her ad agency, and when the job came to an end, instead of pulling out the BlackBerry and mass-copying her resume, she did something a little different: she launched www.hiretina.com, and within weeks she was fielding fabulous job offers, consulting gigs, and more than a few romantic proposals, including an old high-school flame and at least one prison inmate.

How did she do it? Instead of taking the standard route of just posting her resume online and shaking the rolodex for possible positions, Tina set up a website to help *other people* who were looking for work.

Many people have an impression of networking as a negative, self-serving thing, but naturally gifted networkers like Tina intuitively understand that meeting new people and learning about them is fascinating. She's a born socializer and actually takes great pleasure in helping other people, whether it's giving them confidence in their job hunt, hooking them up with tickets to the Packers game, or fixing up Great Aunt Mildred with the retired schoolteacher who accidentally wandered into the under-forty chat room for advertising execs. For Tina, networking isn't so much about how other people can help her; it's about how Tina can help them. (And since Tina is close personal friends with nearly everyone on the planet, she's pretty good at it.) And it would come as no surprise to anyone who's met her that Tina has found herself with a huge network of people who would do practically anything to return a favor.

Tina says, "When I meet somebody online, I always think about other people in the process. I have friends who are looking for other things than I am, and I want to see them happy."

Tina's Rules for Dating

- No date is ever wasted. Approach dating with the idea that you could come out of it with a new client, a new dentist, or a new friend.

- If the chemistry isn't right for you, think about which of your friends might be a good match.

- If you like this person enough to let him through your filter, he'd probably be a great addition to your circle of friends.

- If you don't hit it off, be honest and don't be afraid to say so right away—it's a lot more likely you'll end up as friends if one of you hasn't been strung along.

So if your next date doesn't quite spark, try him on as a friend instead. As for Tina, she's jumped right into a new job she loves. Now she's just in the market for a person to love.

The Man-tidote: Daters Beware

Watch out, ladies, there are a rash of new seduction books for men on the market, offering tips and tricks on how to get a woman in bed without even dating her, let alone investing in a commitment as deep as a cup of coffee.

Now, I'm quite the advocate for good old love and romance, so I think it's pretty important to be able to spot and neutralize these wannabe Casanovas before they pounce.

Whether you want to cut these guys off before they ever make a move or just send the signal that you're not an easy target, we've got the Man-tidote.

Phone Tag and Other Games

The one-night-stand books are generally divided on whether or not to ask for a woman's phone number. One school (or detention center) of thought is that once a guy has gotten what he wanted (sex), there's no reason for getting your phone number. Other books suggest what I like to call the Card Trick—instead of asking for your number, a man will hand you his business card so he doesn't have to go out on the rejection limb and ask for your number.

The Man-tidote: A man who is interested in you will either ask for your phone number or have gained enough information about you during your conversation to get it on his own (through work or mutual friends). If a man hands you his card without asking for your number, simply ask him for a pen, write your number on the back of the card, and return the card to him. That way, he'll not only have your phone number; he'll know that you don't have his (putting the ball back in his court).

Playing the Numbers

Many of these books suggest that a man has better odds of getting sex by hitting on lots of women, with the intention of finding someone who will go for a one-night stand, versus asking a woman for her phone number, then a date, and then campaigning for sex. One book suggests that 20 percent of women in a club are looking for a one-night stand, rationalizing that the remaining 80 percent must be prudish, involved, or, the insecure man's fallback, lesbians.

The Man-tidote: Be part of the 80 percent. Make it a policy not to go for one-night stands.

Whispering in Your Ear

Another tip suggests men whisper in a woman's ear to increase excitement, the excuse, of course, being that the room is loud and he has to whisper for you to hear him. He'll start about nine or ten inches from your ear and gradually move in until his lips are almost touching your ear. While this is an effective way of initiating intimacy, remember that this guy may have an ulterior motive, and that is to get him into position to make his next move.

The Man-tidote: Pull your head away the first time he moves in to whisper, signaling that you're not interested in that level of intimacy with someone you've barely met.

Feeling You Up

As the player moves in for the whisper, he'll be holding his drink in front of his own chest, knuckles outward. As he leans in, he'll brush his knuckles against your breast. This is, of course, all under the guise of being purely unintentional, an accident. If you don't haul off and smack him, he'll take it as a green light to continue "accidentally" touching you every minute or so. In my book, this is the cheap evolution of the cheesy 1950s move that high-school boys made when they pretended to yawn in order to put an arm around a girl at the movies.

The Man-tidote: There are two ways to put a halt to this: with body language (cross your arm in front of your chest, creating both a physical barrier and a strong "blocking" signal) and with words and a knowing look ("Careful, there." or "Yikes! You almost spilled your drink on me.")

"Let's Get Out of Here"

The guiding principal behind most of these books is that the guy will get you so thrilled and giddy with connecting body language and covert touching that you won't have enough time to make a rational decision about whether or not you're interested, and you'll act (and go home with him) from a purely emotional level. When he thinks you might be receptive, he'll ask if he can give you a ride home or if you want to go somewhere else.

The Man-tidote: Don't leave a club, party, or event with someone you've just met. First, it's not safe. Second, your perfect excuse is always, "Sorry, I'm sticking with my girlfriends." And third, if a guy is really interested in dating you, he'll ask for your phone number before he leaves.

Remember, most men are pretty genuine and just as interested in meeting someone special as women are. As for the guys who aren't—well, just be sure to keep your eye out for those sharks in the dating pool.

How to Spot a Baggage Handler

As you probably already know, predators aren't the only potential problems out there. The fact is, any dater over thirty is going to have some emotional baggage. We've all been in relationships before, which colors our outlook now. We see our dates through a filter of hopes and wishes, broken hearts and disappointments, lies and truths, good experiences and bad. But a grown-up dater knows how to handle her own luggage.

Now let's take a look at how you can weed out the men who can't.

Seven Signs He's a Baggage Handler

1. He blatantly flirts with the waitress.

2. He spends the entire date talking about his ex-wife or his ex-girlfriend.

3. He's pretty darn positive that all women are users, liars, and gold diggers.

4. He makes comments that are disrespectful to women.

5. He cheated in his last relationship.

6. He's still married.

7. His finances are a wreck.

In the early stages of dating, it's far easier and more productive to say thank you to a baggage-handling date and move on, rather than trying to date him, fix him, or show him the error of his ways. Now, I'm not saying you should expect your date to be perfect. There's no one on the planet that will fit the bill. But some things that are easy to spot early on (cruelty, cheating, disrespect) will plague the relationship until it ends.

That said, I hear from a lot of women who say every man they date is a jerk. And sometimes it's just a run of bad luck. But sometimes it's a pattern, and the common denominator in all those crappy dates is you.

Letters to Lisa

Dear Lisa,

I can hold it together for anywhere from a few days to a few months, but I get sooooo incredibly insecure that I end up losing it. I mean, I go crazy. I turn into a raging bitch, pick a fight, and think he's doing all kinds of horrible things behind my back, etc. Or I start looking elsewhere and sometimes cheat (which I am embarrassed to admit). All this, if the boyfriend at the time is not falling all over me. I am so insecure. I've been to therapy—still am in therapy. I'm a practicing Christian. I just can't seem to trust a man to save my life. The only thing I've EVER wanted is to get married. I am dating a man right now (for two and a half years). I think we'd be married by now if I hadn't sabotaged the relationship so many times. I mean, he has done some things to damage the relationship, but I think it's mostly been me. I am continuing to work on myself, but sometimes I feel I am beyond help. Any suggestions?

Nightmare Girl

Dearest Reader,

Your letter just broke my heart. First off, please stay in therapy for a while. You're knee-deep in an incredibly destructive pattern right now. For some reason, it seems as though you believe at some level that you don't deserve to be loved, so you sabotage your relationships either by picking unsuitable guys, creating problems, or imagining them. The fact that you believe your boyfriends will treat you badly becomes a self-fulfilling prophecy.

I think part of the reason you think your boyfriends are cheating on you is that you are cheating on them—guilt is a strange, strange thing.

Here's what I think you should do. Stop dating for a while; it seems like it only exacerbates your issues. Give yourself a chance to figure out why you don't believe you deserve to be loved and why you can't trust people. Is it just men? Or is it everybody? If I had to venture a guess in the dark, I'd say you had suffered some sort of abuse, sexual or otherwise. Take a dating sabbatical—give yourself at least six months without a man. In that time, go to therapy and really spend some time figuring out where the pattern started. Take good care of yourself. If you were sexually abused, read The Courage to Heal. *In any case, I want you to realize that you deserve to be loved and treated with respect. Really. You are not damaged goods. You are an amazing, wonderful person. You just need to believe in yourself. And eventually, in someone else.*

Good luck. I'm pulling for you.

Lisa

Let's do a quick check to make sure you're not practicing any self-sabotaging dating behaviors. If you are, don't worry—below you'll find some tips to help you get you back on track.

Seven Signs You're Handling Some Baggage

1. You sleep with men sooner than you plan to.

   Give up the baggage: Make a policy not to sleep with a man for at least two months. If you need to tape your knees together or buy a chastity belt to make it happen, by all means, do it. Otherwise, stick to group dates until you're out of the danger zone.

2. You want to hurry up and get married so you can start your "real life."

   Give up the baggage: Live the life you imagine *right now*—if you knew you were going to be single for the rest of your life, what would you do differently? Travel? Get a different job? Stop waiting for tomorrow; live the life you dream of today.

3. Men are jerks, unless proven otherwise.

   Give up the baggage: Some men are jerks, and so are some women. Don't assume your next date is like your last date. It's not fair, and it's not helping.

4. You cheated in your last relationship.

   Give up the baggage: Whether it was insecurity, general misery, or impulse control, you can't expect to find a good partner if you aren't a good partner. Be one.

5. You don't want to waste time with a relationship that isn't going anywhere, so you press for a commitment, or at least a statement of his general intentions, by the third date.

   Give up the baggage: There is nothing that sends a man running for the door faster than a woman sizing him up for marriage potential. You're not as subtle as you think—he knows what you're up to.

6. You want to meet his family and friends right away.

    Give up the baggage: This is one of many signs of try-
    ing to rush the relationship into something more seri-
    ous. Unfortunately, by doing that, you're actually slowing
    things down, because the guy feels like he has to put on
    the brakes all the time. Let him pace the relationship, and
    it will move more quickly.

7. Rather than simply enjoying your dates, getting to know
    them, and falling in love naturally, you're far more inter-
    ested in fitting them for flaws and locking them into the
    Two-Year Groom Timeline. *(Sign up today, and we'll throw
    in these lovely monogrammed towels!)*

    Give up the baggage: This is a symptom of looking for
    a husband rather than a partner, and no man wants to be
    lucky winner #237 of an all-expenses-paid trip down the
    aisle. Focus on the moment and the experience of each
    date, not the outcome.

If you are reading this list and realizing that you might be the
baggage handler, it's time to take stock and change the dating
behavior that's holding you back.

You have two options here: you can keep doing the same thing
and getting the same results (and you're waaaay too smart for
that), or you can make some changes.

Most women have a sort of laundry list of the things they're
looking for in a man—tall, well-mannered, kind, handy with a
wrench, willing to kill bugs, generous, and faithful. But you have
to be the partner you want.

With the exception of bug killing, take a good, long look at
your list and cross off any personality traits you couldn't claim

for yourself. If you're suspicious, damaged, selfish, and wary of the opposite sex, you will inevitably attract partners who are the same.

Conversely, if you are kind, generous, loving, and trustworthy, you'll find yourself dating a nicer group of men.

Every woman has felt the feelings you're feeling. We've all made those mistakes at one time or another.

I'm rooting for you. I think you're brave to keep trying for what you want, even if it comes more slowly than you'd like. I want you to win, find a wonderful guy, and live your own version of happily ever after. And it breaks my heart when I see women sabotage their own efforts to find love.

Think about how you approach dating, and figure out a way that you can go into a date with an open mind and an open heart.

Most of all, let go of the things that are holding you back.

Letters to Lisa ♥♥♥♥♥♥♥♥

Dear Lisa,

About nine months ago, I ended a four-year relationship. It was a very violent and abusive relationship (if you even want to call it that), and I am still a little shaken up. I tried the Cupid.com dating service and met a seemingly really great guy. We have been corresponding by email for about a week now. I think he wants to meet me, but I'm not sure if I should. I don't want to ruin my chance with the online guy because I'm still not secure. I'm really afraid that I'll end up with another guy like my ex, and I can't—no, won't—go through that again. What should I do? Take my chances or hide? Please lend me an ear; I'm sort of on my own in this. Thank you.

Writing Scared

Dear Scared,

After prying yourself free from an abusive relationship, it's no wonder you're a bit dating-shy. This is your brain protecting the rest of you. This is a good thing.

I'm glad you're concerned about ending up in the same situation, because frequently women who have endured abusive relationships end up repeating the pattern. I'm worried about you, too. You don't want to end up with a newer version of the same jerk.

One week might be a bit soon to meet someone face-to-face, and you need to make sure that you feel comfortable before taking any further steps. You also need to make sure that if you do decide to meet with him face-to-face, you take along a friend (or three) for support and safety.

Pay attention to what the little voice is telling you. If any man you're dating begins to exhibit signs of abusiveness (jealousy, controlling behavior, nastiness), hit the road and don't look back. You know from experience that an abuser will never change, so don't give bad behavior the chance to escalate.

I'd suggest you talk with a therapist or go to a support group to talk through what you've been through, and give yourself a support system so that you don't end up falling into another relationship that isn't good for you.

That said, you don't want to live your life in fear. Trust your instincts, but don't hide under the covers. Just remember you're an amazing, special person worthy of respect and love, and don't settle until you find that. You deserve it. If you're feeling a bit unsteady, just slow things down a bit. Any guy worth his salt will respect your wishes and go along at whatever pace you feel comfortable with.

Believe in yourself, and know that someday, you'll be able to believe in others again. There are good guys out there. Trust me.

Hugs,

Lisa

The Dating Mommy: How to Date When You're Single With Kids

I was flipping through the channels the other day, and I got sucked into one of those sappy, made-for-cable movies in which an attractive woman finds herself the single mother of two adorable small children after her husband has died tragically or run off with the town tramp. The first thing I wondered was how a woman living alone with two young kids managed the upkeep on her Heather Locklear-esque blonde highlights. (For some reason, they never cut to the scene where the kids were emptying out bottles of nail polish and shredding magazines in the waiting room while their foil-covered mother cowered in embarrassment under a dryer.) The second thing I noticed was that she had no problem at all meeting men in chance encounters at funerals, at the gas station, or at her sister's place of business (all of whom, of course, were more than delighted to date a single mom). And last, the children (who during daylight hours were the center of Mom's universe) conveniently vaporized after sunset so as not to spoil her big (but unplanned, because that would be too trampy) night of romance.

As a tear-jerking diversion from reality and a plausible excuse to eat cookie dough right out of the tube, such movies are top-notch. But as any single parent will tell you, the reality of dating is quite a bit different. Single moms frequently feel like dowdy, second-class daters, simply because they have children. Many single women believe they can't compete for the really great men, because most men won't want a woman with somebody else's children, and they don't typically have the time or money to spend on the elaborate clothes/hair/makeup routines of their childless counterparts.

Add to that the date-scheduling challenge of custody arrangements (every other weekend and alternate Tuesdays), having to cancel at the last minute because a babysitter doesn't show, and being physically and emotionally spent (and possibly covered in Cheerios) before your date has even begun, it's a miracle we ever attempt to leave the house, let alone date, at all. But while juggling dating and day care may not be as easy as trolling the bars in your carefree youth, it can be done, and it can be fun.

Parent-Friendly Dating Options

After drive-thru and DVD players in the car, the greatest boon to busy single moms is online dating (more on this in Chapter 7). Why? With online dating, you can search out Mr. Fabulous at 2:00 a.m., weed out anybody who's not kid friendly, and flirt a little (or a lot) while your offspring are tucked safely in their beds. You can test the waters via email before you commit to an actual night out. Plus, thanks to your fabulous date-ready photo, no one ever needs to know that you're flirting away in a ketchup-stained shirt and bunny slippers.

Other parent-friendly options? Parents without Partners (www.parentswithoutpartners.org) offers social events for single moms and dads, and fish-in-the-barrel approaches like speed dating offer a quick way to meet lots of potential dates in one swift evening. You can knock out forty dates in one night (and one outfit) and be home before the eleven o'clock news. (See Chapter 6 for more on speed dating.)

Dating Guidelines for Single Parents

- If scheduling a date in between soccer practice, homework, and dinner is a challenge, try meeting for lunch or coffee instead.

- Don't spend the entire date talking about your kids, even though they're really amazing. For a first date, names and ages only. After that you can add five minutes of kid talk each date. (That's five minutes on the second date, ten minutes on the third date, etc.) When you get to thirty minutes, stop.

- Avoid the Parade of Uncles. Make sure you know your date very well before you consider introducing him to your children. Why? Children form attachments quickly, and it's traumatic for them when the person disappears, especially when it happens over and over again every few months. Eventually, the kids learn not to trust in relationships, that the people they care for are not permanent. (A lesson already implanted when Mom and Dad got divorced.)

- Gradually introduce your date to your children in a short, family-oriented activity, such as a picnic or a baseball game.

- If your kids don't like your date, listen to and carefully evaluate their reasons why. Never force your kids to spend time with your date alone.

- Don't sacrifice time with your kids for time with your dates. They need you more.

- Until you get remarried, don't have sleepovers when your kids are around. Inconvenient, but necessary.

- If your date has kids also, don't jump into introducing your children too early. Wait several months before making an introduction, until the time when you feel the relationship has a pretty strong chance of becoming permanent.

"The biggest mistake parents make is introducing their kids to the new person too early," says Lisa Earle McLeod, author of *Forget Perfect*. "The *Brady Bunch* fantasy you have about your new family unit is entirely in your head."

Remember, if your date can't roll with last-minute schedule changes, covert sleepovers that rival CIA missions, and more than a few rounds at Chuck E. Cheese, don't take the plunge with him.

And if you are a single parent, remember it's your experience with your kids that has made you into the person you are today: Someone who is capable of great love. Someone who knows the meaning of responsibility. Someone who is making a contribution to the world. In other words, a great catch.

How to Break It to Your (Adult) Kids That You Have a Better Social Life Than They Do

This part is for those of you with grown children.

Many of you are uncomfortable about telling your kids that you're dating again, especially when you have an unmarried adult daughter.

You're both going to have to get over yourselves.

Sit her down when you're both in a good mood, and tell her kindly and matter-of-factly that you've started dating again.

You are an adult; you deserve to be happy; and the matter is not up for discussion. Don't discuss your sex life (or intentions for a sex life)—that is no one's business but yours.

Sometimes when daughters get upset about the idea of their mother having a social life, it's because of their own fears that they will never meet someone. (Or if it's serious, that they'll be written out of the will.) Reassure your daughter that she is a wonderful person and that she will meet someone great. (And if you're so inclined, reassure her about your will.)

The Grown-Up Bottom Line: You're an adult, and you'll make your own decisions about your social life.

That said, if your daughter, son, or friend has serious doubts about someone in particular that you are dating, pay attention: They probably have your best interests at heart, and they may see something you don't.

The good news is that a lot of women worry, obsess, and generally make themselves crazy about having "the talk" with their kids, and when they drop the big news, the kids are mildly enthusiastic, but generally unconcerned.

Chapter 6

43 Dates in a Night: How to Speed Date

Slow Down, You Move Too Fast

In a world of eight-minute abs and one-minute managers, it's no surprise that three-minute dates would soon follow. Speed dating (sometimes called PreDating) is still one of the hottest dating trends in the country. Why the appeal? It's hilarious; you can do it with your friends; and it's loads of fun. It's kind of like musical chairs for grown-ups.

Here's how it works: Women sit at numbered tables, and men join them for a three- to ten-minute mini-date. You chat, you smile, you flip your hair; then the buzzer sounds, and your three-minute man moves to the next table. You both check yes or no on your scorecard, and the beat goes on. A new guy sits down, and you do it all over again. At the end of the night, everybody turns in their scorecard, and the organizers send you an email a few days later that gives you contact information for all the people that you liked who also liked you.

The great news is that three minutes is really all it takes to judge whether or not we'd like to see someone again. Studies at the University of California–Berkley showed that we can predict with about 80 percent accuracy how a relationship will turn out (friendship, romance, sneaking out the bathroom window) within the first three minutes.

In an average night of speed dating, you can go on about forty dates without breaking a sweat. Better than that, most people make an average of six matches. Which means you end up with six people you like who also like you. Not too bad for an evening's play.

The drawback, of course, is that there's not much chance to make a good second impression if you blow your first one. Given that, here are some tips to give you that va-va-voom right from the get-go.

Smile

There's no quicker way to improve your looks and make a great impact than to smile. Psychology and body-language experts agree that it's one of the most effective ways to make yourself more attractive and approachable. It's not necessary to do your most convincing game-show spokesmodel impression—just your usual "I'm having a great time, and I'm happy to be here" face will do the trick.

The Color Cue

If you want to create an on-the-spot thrill, wearing red is the way to go. (Yes, I know, I'm repeating myself here, but this particular tip is really effective in this particular situation.) According to color experts, the most stimulating color you can wear is red, which actually increases blood flow. (And mimics attraction.)

While you might have some concerns about the men you'll attract while wearing red in other social situations (see Chapter 2), speed dating is not one of them. You have a very short time in which to make an indelible impression, and va-va-voom red does the trick.

How to Score

Be sure to write the person's name next to his number. That way if you get mixed up somehow (don't feel bad—it happens all the time), it will be easier for organizers to figure out what's what and who's who. Be sure to keep your scorecard facedown on the table during your date; nobody else needs to know if you're the most selective person on the planet or you're just playing the odds, hoping for the big winner. And—this should go without saying—don't score your date while he's still at the table.

Grown-Up Dating Fact

Most men use more of an "elimination strategy" and choose many women when speed dating, but most women choose just a few men.

First Things First

Get any deal breakers out of the way right away. Hate smokers? Ask now if he'll be looking for an ashtray on the break. Horribly allergic to cats? Find out quick if he's a magnet for four-legged strays. You'll save yourself some trouble later if you get the deal breakers out on the table.

Where Are You From? What Do You Do?

Try to avoid asking the same old boring questions that everyone else is asking. By the time someone has asked you what you do for a living thirty-four times, it's bound to be pretty stale. Ask questions that are fun or unusual (but not bizarre), and humor is always good. Not only will you find out something interesting about your date, but you'll stand out in his mind as well.

Good: What would your best friend say about you?

Bad: If you were an axe murderer, where would you keep the bodies?

The good news is that you don't have to come up with an original question for every date—you can just pick one or two, and use them over and over again.

Keep It Clean

A three-minute conversation—or even a ten-minute chat—isn't long enough to bring up sex. Really.

If your date says something inappropriate (it doesn't happen often, but some people just don't know how to behave), let the organizer know at the break so she can take care of the issue.

The Safety Drill

The good news about speed dating is that you pay for the event online via credit card, so you have a pretty good idea that your date is who he says he is. Once you've made a few matches and you decide to meet for a date, remember to always meet in a public place or even in a group-date setting, and use the same precautions you'd use for meeting an online date.

Which Company Does It Best?

There are a variety of speed-dating companies that operate in the same basic way—the main difference is the length of the dates. Eight-Minute Dating (www.8minutedating.com) offers fewer dates with a longer time (eight minutes) for each date. Fast Dater (www.fastdater.com) offers three minutes, so you'll meet about forty people in one night, and PreDating (www.predating. com) dates are about four to six minutes, so you'll meet around twenty to twenty-five people in one two- to three-hour event. All the companies listed above hold events nationwide.

SpeedDating (www.speeddating.com), the originator of speed dating, holds events targeted to Jewish singles, and other smaller, local and regional companies have offerings as well. If you prefer to go with a small local company, just search online for "speed dating [YOUR CITY]."

Personally, I tend to favor the companies that feature shorter dates with more people. Remember, it only takes three minutes to figure out if you want to see someone again, and if you don't, eight minutes can seem just too damned long.

Letters to Lisa

Dear Lisa,

I've been dating my boyfriend for five months. At first I was extremely secure, because he was always emailing me at work, and it was always guaranteed that I would see him during the week. But I've noticed in the past month that he is more moody and not as reliable about emails and hanging out during the week. This behavior has made me start to feel insecure, which in turn has made me act very insecure. He has told me time and time again that I have nothing to be insecure about and that he loves me dearly. Still, though, I come across as needy. Not calling or emailing seems impossible at times, because that is something we have always done. I feel that this man could be the one for me, but I don't want to turn a good relationship sour with my neediness.

Losing It

Dear Losing It,

Here's what's happening. Your guy is telling you by his actions that he needs a little space. You are freaking out and reacting to this by becoming clingy, asking for constant reassurance, and in fact, YOU ARE GIVING HIM LESS SPACE. Here's what will happen if you don't quit. He'll back off a bit, and you'll chase him down. Then he'll back off a bit more, and you'll chase him down again. Repeat, repeat, repeat, until he makes a break for it.

If you stop chasing after him, he'll stop running away. Here's what you need to do: Don't initiate contact with him, but do reply to his emails. He won't think you're being manipulative and mean—he'll think he's dating a wonderfully secure girl who can respect his needs for a little extra distance once in a while.

While you're at it, make some plans for next weekend to hang out with your girlfriends. Your guy cannot (and should not) be solely responsible for your entire social agenda.

Best,

Lisa

Chapter 7

I Thought You'd Be Taller: Navigating the World of Online Dating

The Fastest-Growing Group of Online Daters Is Over Forty

Nearly 30 percent of those born between 1946 and 1964 are single, and many are actively looking for love. In fact, millions of them are doing it from the comfort of their laptops.

There are some great things about online dating: you can go out on a date with an attractive, interesting person every night of the week; you can meet someone who shares your adoration of cheesy sitcoms, gossipy tabloids, or argyle sweater vests; and you can order up sex just as easily as a pepperoni pizza.

But online dating also brings out the nastiest parts of dating as well: people who lie, email breakups, and the hopeless distraction that we sometimes feel when our soul mate seems utterly out of reach.

The good news is that you're not alone. Men and women over forty are flocking to online dating sites by the thousands. So not only will you have a lot of company, but many sites, such as Lavalife Prime (www.prime.lavalife.com), Match.com (www.match.com), YourTimeSingles.com (www.yourtimesingles.com), and SeniorFriendFinder.com (www.seniorfriendfinder.com)

specifically cater to the over-forty crowd. (See page 100 for more on picking a site.)

What's a girl to do? Sit back and relax, and I'll break down the basics for you.

Hyperdating: How Online Dating Speeds Up the Courting Process

Many people who brave the scene have honed their online dating skills to an exact science. The scenario goes something like this:

You meet online. Something sparks and you find yourself emailing back and forth like a couple of lovesick teenagers. You share your traumatic frog experience from the fourth grade; he confesses that his favorite song is "Wind Beneath My Wings."

Before you know it, you're trading photos, rapid-firing IMs, and setting a date for coffee/lunch/drinks. You finally meet in person, decide the chemistry just isn't enough to overcome your previous knowledge of his cat collection/persistent underemployment/sketchy wardrobe, and you end the date before the waiter has a chance to bring a check. Or there is a spark, and you bond feverishly over your previously established adoration of canned ravioli/Graham Norton/tarot cards. In which case, you finish your apple-tinis (certain you've found your soul mate) and head back to your place.

Unfortunately, looking for something meaningful can be a challenge in the convenience-driven world of online dating. Why settle for less than romance-novel perfection when there is a full menu of replacement dates as close as the nearest Internet connection? And with the introduction of mobile dating (dating via cell phone) now here, industrious daters can be hooking up with someone new while their not-so-fantastic date is in the restaurant bathroom. Ten years ago, a date meant drinks, dinner, and a movie. Today, it means the same thing—but with three different people.

Welcome to the turbo version of online dating: hyperdating and the thirty-minute mini-date. Contrary to what you might expect, most hyperdaters aren't slutty, sex-crazed players looking for a hookup. In fact, many daters use hyperdating as a way to speed up the traditional dating process in order to find a meaningful relationship.

Here's the good news: thanks to the magic of romance technology and round-the-clock man shopping, you can cram fifteen years' worth of dating into a mere thirty-seven months. The bad news: you may be so numb from chronic overdating that you fail to realize when Mr. Right finally hits your inbox.

How to Make Hyperdating Pay Off

More good news: You can learn from somebody's profile what would have taken Grandma five dates to glean in a traditional dating process. The bad news: We make instant assessments— too short, too lazy, too undereducated. In a slower-paced social setting like Grandma's—or with repeated contact because you work for the same company, go to the same church, or hang out with the same friends—you might take the time to get to know someone who wouldn't fit your ideal profile: somebody bad on paper, and great in person. In the efficiency-driven world of on-line dating, it's easier to make snap judgments based on height, job description, and pet preference. Like the millionaire in a scruffy jacket and torn blue jeans who's passed over by the Lexus salesman, a shopper who doesn't look like he can make the payments doesn't get offered the test drive.

The solution? While hyperdating can certainly increase your odds of meeting someone fabulous a lot faster, it can also make it more of a challenge to make a real connection. The key is to take a deep breath and make an effort to go beyond the profile and photo and get to know the real person. *In* person.

In the end, it doesn't matter if it's your fourth date of the day, fourth date of the month, or even fourth date of your whole life. Every person you meet is a chance to meet "the one." The key is to keep your eyes, your heart, and your mind open. And remember, while online dating has its perks, you can't hurry love.

How to Choose an Online Dating Site

There are hundreds, if not thousands, of online dating sites to choose from, so how do you pick the one that's right for you?

If you're looking for a marriage partner, try eHarmony.com, as it tends to attract more commitment-minded members. If religion, politics, or pets are important to you, there are a variety of niche sites that will help you find someone with similar values (try CatholicSingles.com, RepublicanSingles.us, Democratsingles. com, or do a search online for whatever you're looking for). If you live in New York, the site of choice is JDate.com—and even if you're not Jewish, JDate has a large New York member base. And if you're considering one of the general dating sites, PlentyofFish.com is the largest free site in the world, and Match. com and Lavalife.com have members in the millions. One of my favorites is Cupid.com, which partners with local radio stations. The reason I like this site in particular is that you have clusters of singles in the same geographic area who listen to the same radio station. (And generally people who like the same types of music have other things in common as well.)

How to Pick the Perfect Online Dating Site for You

If you'd like some help to sort through the thousands of online dating sites to figure out what will work best for you, there's an online-dating site-match tool at LisaDaily.com to help you find the best site for you, based on your dating goals.

Just answer a few questions about what you're looking for (companionship or marriage, someone to travel with, political preferences, someone who shares your same interests, etc.), and the site-match tool will pair you with the best sites to fit your needs. Enter the code GROWNUP to use the tool for free as often as you'd like.

Working My Way Back to You, Babe

Sites like Classmates.com, Reunion.com, and FindClassmates-ForFree.com can help you track down the guy who sat behind you in Biology 101 in tenth grade and have been incredibly popular for men and women looking to connect with lost loves online. While it's great to have a blast from the past and those relationships can sometimes result in romance, it's important to remember that you can't just pick up where you left off in 1973. You've done a lot of living since then (see page 43 for more on hooking up with old flames).

Making Online Dating Work for You

Does online dating really work? Sure, it does. Of course there's always a possibility of meeting the *Star Trek* troll who lives with his mother (or worse, other *Star Trek* trolls). The prison inmate. The forgot-to-mention-he's-married guy. But for the most part, online dating is still a great way to meet someone.

Whether you're new to the dating game entirely or just looking for a refresher, here are some tips on how to make online dating work for you.

Honesty Counts

Online daters with the best luck are those who are honest in their profiles and pictures. That means being honest about your job, your marital status, and your age. It also means posting a recent, accurate photo—not a twelve-year-old picture of you with more hair, fewer laugh lines, and twenty fewer pounds. There's nothing that puts a damper on a date like the bait and switch. Don't worry; you look better than you think.

Letters to Lisa ♥♥♥♥♥♥♥

Dear Lisa,

I'm not beautiful. I wouldn't even call myself attractive, but I am smart, and I have a great sense of humor. I have begun to date online, and I'm wondering if I should avoid posting an online photo. Men are such visual creatures, and I think I'd have a better chance if they got to know me first. What do you think?

Beauty on the Inside

Dear Beauty,

First of all, you may be being too hard on yourself when it comes to your looks. Many of us feel that we're not as attractive as we'd like to be. You may be so-so; you may be one of those elegant women who doesn't even know it; or you may be absolutely right. Whatever the truth is, it's important to remember two things: (1) beauty is in the eye of the beholder (so one man's Mack-truck accident is another man's Ferrari); and (2) there are several someones for everyone.

I would advise you to go ahead and post your most charming photo of yourself (ask a male friend to help you pick one—women are attracted to different things than men are). I wouldn't skip the photo altogether, because nobody wants to end up with the big online-dating surprise package. You're right: men are very visual, but your odds go down dramatically if you don't post a picture or two. Most people won't even look at online profiles that don't include a picture.

Put your best self forward; let that fabulous sense of humor or brilliant mind shine. It's what's inside the package, and not the wrapping, that counts.

Hugs,

Lisa

A Picture's Worth a Thousand Emails

This is possibly your most important asset in successful online dating. Most people will pass by a photo-free profile, no matter how fabulous it may be. Dating is all about chemistry, and nobody wants to end up with whoever is behind door number three. Four quick tips:

- **Put Your Best Face Forward:** Make sure your photo features the best possible picture of you.

- **Crop It:** Feel free to crop to get the best shot, and pump up the contrast to add a little excitement. (Try it. It adds an extra va-va-voom, and you'll just pop off the page.)

- **Go It Alone:** Avoid using pictures of you and other people, even if the other people are blurred out. The message you're trying to send is "fun," "sexy," or "interesting," not "witness protection program."

- **Get Their Hearts Racing with Red:** Wear red in your photo, or use a red background. It automatically makes you stand out from the crowd and seem more exciting.

Be a Snapshot Detective! How to Read an Online Photo

A girlfriend of mine regularly emails me to check out the latest eligible guy she's spotted online. I've known her for a long time, and I know that as perfect a match as he may be personality-wise, a dark-haired, scrawny guy is a no-go, while any Nordic, Howie Long look-alikes are a shoo-in for at least a bit of email flirting, even if they have B.O. that smells like old socks and garlic or the IQ of a house cat.

Generally, when we're looking at someone's online photo, we're looking at the picture from the standpoint of pure, basic chemistry—are we attracted? But an online photo offers more than just a baseline measure of looks; it offers a little peek into the soul. And unlike lightning-fast gestures or expressions we might encounter on a date, the online photo can be studied for all its subtle nuances.

- Someone who is posting a variety of photos (formal and casual, with friends and alone) is invested in the process of online dating, and is probably truly interested in finding a relationship.

- Most people don't trust professionally done "glamour shots"—they wonder what's going on under the airbrushing.

- People with fewer friends in their photos tend to be more serious or introverted; more friends generally mean the person is more extroverted.

- The background of a photo can offer lots of personality clues, from artwork preferences to clutter comfort.

Letters to Lisa

Dear Lisa,

I am afraid to post my photo online. I am in an unhappy relationship right now and am afraid if my other half sees my photo, there might be trouble. There is one guy who has viewed my profile, and I am very interested in him—but how can I get to know him more, when I am afraid to post my photo?

Camera Shy

Dear Camera Shy,

Hmmm. What to do, what to do? You can't post a photo online for the purpose of online dating, because your current boyfriend might see it. But you can't take things to the next level with your new love interest, because there's no way he's committing to the mystery date he's never seen before.

Here's a thought: Break up with your boyfriend before starting to date anyone else. Call me crazy, but it just might work.

If you're unhappy, why are you hanging on to him?

Best,

Lisa

The Profile: Your Round-the-Clock Matchmaker

Your profile is your second most important tool. Five quick tips:

1. Use advertising principles to create immediate interest and action. Here's what you need to create a profile that pulls: a snappy headline, three key points (it's not a resume, darling; it's small talk), and a big finish (known to advertising people as a "call to action").

2. Avoid bad puns, clichés, and pitiful jokes, such as "Go ahead, click my day" or anything that sounds desperate, such as "Are You Prince Charming?" or "Searching for Soul Mate."

3. Funny is good, and frankly, nothing works better than humor or a compelling question to intrigue others and bring those eligibles flying into your inbox. Here are some interesting options:

   • "Outdoorswoman seeking good catch."

   • "The girl below me is a stalker."

   • "Should people wear socks to the beach?"

- "Am I the only woman on the planet who can't stand cats?"

Most people will click on a profile with a funny title just to see what the person has to say next.

4. Men love to quote guy-movie lines, so if you're a fan of *The Godfather, Caddyshack, Apocalypse Now, Airplane, A Few Good Men, Dirty Harry,* or *Blazing Saddles,* your favorite man-movie line makes a good opener and a way to make an instant connection.

   - "Cinderella story. Outta nowhere. A former greens keeper, now, about to become the Masters champion."

   - "I love the smell of napalm in the morning."

   - "Don't call me Shirley."

   - "The question you have to ask yourself is, 'Do you feel lucky?' Well, do ya punk?"

   - "A wed wose; how womantic."

   - "Badges? We don't need no stinking badges."

5. And last but not least, SPELL-CHECK! The technology is there; all you have to do is push the button.

Grown-Up Dating Fact

Before going out on a first date, 57 percent of singles may say to themselves the date will be a waste of time. Yet 42 percent are optimistic and feel every date could be an opportunity to meet "the one."

Source: Colgate Simply White Dating Survey

Email Suave

Once your virtual want ad is up and running, you're ready to make contact. Emailing a potential date is like flirting. You want to captivate without giving everything away. Both humor and intrigue are great ways to break the ice and send those sparks burning over the DSL. Start off your email with something like, "I noticed the most interesting thing about you." Don't spill what the interesting thing was; just use it as a teaser. He won't know if it's his haiku profile or his in-depth knowledge of macramé that snagged you. People are fundamentally curious. It will gnaw at him until he writes back—and bingo, you've got contact.

Once again, it's important to keep your emails snappy—short and funny. Go into too much depth, and you'll induce your online Romeo to snores. In-depth analysis of your feelings is what therapy is for—this, ladies, is flirting.

It's usually best to avoid hot-button subjects like politics, abortion, and gun control until after you know each other a bit better. Also, don't complain about your parade of exes and how the opposite sex is out to get you. (If you feel that way, you need to take a little sabbatical and get some *real* therapy before you wade back in to the dating pool.) It's also a good idea to keep your email contact balanced—try to match him one for one. In other words, don't send four emails to his one. You'll come off as being a bit overzealous.

Your Date Is Not Your Therapist

On a related note, remember that while your life experiences can help you to form a real connection, your date is not your therapist. Keep it light and positive. No droning on about horrifying ex-spouses or ungrateful kids. If you've just been through a difficult experience like a divorce or a breakup, your impulse may be to spill your story to the first guy who will listen. Don't. (Unless that guy is your therapist.)

Men Don't "Get" Cats

I know you love your cat(s). They're fabulous animals. In the world of online dating, however, cats are a big red flag for a man.

So until you get to know him better, lay off on the "love me, love my cats" talk, the 673 pictures of Mr. Fluffkins in his vacation wardrobe that are currently sprucing up your online profile, and the incessant cat chat. He'll meet Mr. Fluffkins soon enough. And while photos of you and your big, man-friendly dog can actually attract a guy's attention to your profile, photos of cats and small, cat-sized dogs (anything that fits in a handbag counts) can actually drive men away.

Seven Sins of Online Dating

Many of you reading this will have been on at least a few (or a few hundred) online dates. And with more than forty million of people dating online, sifting through all the thousands of profiles to find your perfect match can be quite a challenge. The key is in dating smart and making your profile stand out from all the others, while avoiding the online dating mistakes that cause potential suitors to skip your profile.

Read below, my little love disciples. Are you committing one of the seven deadly sins of online dating?

Sin #1: Thou Shalt Not Wear Chartreuse

As we've discussed, many color experts believe that chartreuse (yellowish-green) is one color that actually repels both men and women. So even if you're the rare person who looks good in fluorescent Slurpee-green, don't wear it in your photos or on your date. You're not doing yourself any favors.

Sin #2: Thou Shalt Not Forget to Post a Photo

It's a fact. Profiles that include photos get eight times more responses. It's also important to remember that lots of people won't even consider dating someone without a photo. Pictures are the quickest way to show off your looks and your personality and crank up your online dating odds.

Be sure your photo is up-to-date: Since physical attraction is a big part of love, you want to find someone who's attracted to you right now. Not someone who is attracted to you fifteen pounds lighter and seven years younger. With different hair. And one less tattoo.

Sin #3: Thou Shalt Not Give Out Too Much Personal Information

Robert Siciliano, CEO of IDTheftSecurity.com, says, "Online dating is the textbook definition of the blind date. The biggest mistakes people make are giving out their first and last name and then giving out their home or cell phone number. With these pieces of information, anyone can find out where you live, and they have enough data to compromise your identity. The Internet has made it extremely easy for a person to be searched via home phone, cell phone, and name. Purposefully or inadvertently giving out a home address is never a good idea until you are positive this is a sane person you want to spend time with. If you're going to give a phone number, give out a nontraceable number." Services such as MyPrivateLine.com can make it easier to keep your personal information to yourself.

Another word to the wise: If you have children, it is a bad idea to post photographs of them with your profile or email such photos later on. It's just not safe.

Sin #4: Thou Shalt Not Search for an Exact Duplicate of Yourself (Thyself?)

Having some common interests is great, but don't insist your personalities be matchy-matchy. It shouldn't be a requirement that you find someone who loves all of the same things you do. Why? Even a classics-loving vegetarian cyclist can find happiness with a hard-rock-ballad-crazy, romance-novel-reading steak lover. As long as you have shared values and your personalities click, your Sunday-evening activity preference isn't nearly so important. No matter how compatible you are, men and women generally like different things. You can always go antique shopping with your girlfriends.

Sin #5: Thou Shalt Not Lie

Ahh, the biggest of all dating sins. The problem with saying you're twenty-seven when you're forty-seven, claiming you look like Julia Roberts when you really look like Julie Andrews, or bragging that you own the building when you're actually the janitor, is that once you meet in person, you're probably going to be exposed. Not only will you tick off the person who is really searching for the twenty-seven-year-old real-estate mogul/Julia Roberts look-alike, you'll also likely miss out on the person who's looking for a mature, Julie Andrews-ish woman who's handy around the house. You'll never find the perfect person for you if you're pretending to be someone else. Give you a chance.

Sin #6: Thou Shalt Not Eliminate a Potential Date Based Solely on a Bad Phone Call

You meet online; you whip out a few intriguing emails; and when you're buzzing with anticipation, you schedule that first magical phone call. And it's, um, odd. Suddenly, you don't have as much to talk about. Where have all the sparks gone? One telephone conversation, and you've hit the skids? Never fear, and go ahead and make that date anyway.

Men are generally not as good on the phone as women are, especially when they're nervous. At least meet for coffee.

Sin #7: Thou Shalt Not Cancel a First Date

Now, this isn't to say you can't turn down a first date and then go on to have a great date at another time. If you already have plans, there's no need to break them for Mr. or Miss Possibly Fabulous, unless you really want to. However, if you make a date and then break it, your date is inclined to believe that something better came along or that you just weren't interested. Yet another reason not to cancel a first date: Most people won't give you a second chance; they'll move on.

Are you guilty of committing a few online dating sins? Well, don't beat yourself up about it. The beautiful thing about online dating (and life) is that you get a fresh start every day.

Dating Like a Grown-Up—Online

As we discussed in Chapter 5, I am basically an old-fashioned girl. Well, sort of. Actually, I'm one of those new modern-woman/old-fashioned-girl hybrids—the stiletto feminist. You know, a take-no-prisoners, hard-ass over-achiever at the office and an ultra girly-girl at heart.

A lot of women are just like me. We grew up with moms and grandmas and aunts who told us never to call a boy and that a gentleman should always hold open the door for a lady and offer to pay for dinner. Of course, these same moms and aunts also went to the office, clawing and fighting for equal rights. They succeeded in raising daughters (and frequently sons) who understood that women could be fabulously successful at work but still hold onto the dream of an elegant, old-fashioned sweetheart of a guy who would toss his jacket over a puddle so we wouldn't ruin our Christian Louboutins, call us midweek to schedule a weekend dinner date, and squash (or at least relocate to the patio) any six-legged creatures that happened to find their way into the kitchen.

So although we old-fashioned girls (OFGs) feel pretty much at home while being aggressive superwomen at the office, many of us get a little bit squeamish when it comes to making the first move with regard to online romance. When faced with the idea of approaching a man first, we feel weird. We feel desperate. We feel, uh, trampy.

And frankly, we OFGs are not entirely off base when it comes to our mind-set about being the romantic aggressor. A survey of men over the last two years reveals that most men enjoy it when a woman pursues them, but they also believe that there is ultimately something wrong with a woman who makes the first move and perceive her to be either desperate or an easy target for sex. Of course, there are always exceptions to the rule. Some men (darlings, aren't they?) could care less about who makes the first move.

However, when it comes to online dating, we OFGs may be at a bit of a disadvantage to our less-traditional and more-pursuant counterparts. After all, while we are sprucing up our profiles, creating just the right video message, polishing our email repartee, and waiting for Mr. Right to track us down, our go-get-em sisters are busy scouting eligibles and whipping out email and IM banter.

If you're the type of woman who never calls a man, is it the same thing if you email him? Is sending a "smile" the equivalent to batting your eyelashes at a guy at a party or more like buying him a double tequila shooter and telling him you have a tattoo you want to show him in private?

The fact is, online dating isn't like regular dating. When Grandma handed down the fourth commandment of romance to never call a man, she had no idea the future would hold anything as wild as online dating. And now that she's back in the dating pool, she's just as perplexed about what "counts" and what doesn't as the rest of us OFGs. Email or not to email? Meet or not to meet? "Smile" or not to "smile"?

The Grown-Up Bottom Line: Go ahead and send a little a spark to that guy you've been eyeing. Generally speaking, I think it's a more effective strategy to let the man make the first move, but online dating is such a big, wide world, sometimes it's hard to tell if you're even on his radar.

Send a wink or a nod or your online dating site's gimmick of choice, but leave the first email contact to the guys (that way they'll feel like the pursuers, even if you spotted them first.) From that point on, you can simply respond to his emails.

You never know—maybe he's been looking for an old-fashioned girl exactly like you.

Letters to Lisa ♥♥♥♥♥♥♥♥

Dear Lisa,

I must really be doing something wrong, because I have been online dating for a while now and have been dumped a lot.

I don't like to get too serious with anyone (well, not at first). Then later, when I try to step things up, they tell me they've found someone else. I don't know if you hear stories like this from other guys—maybe it's just me. Is there any advice you can give me?

Not Clicking

Dear Clicking,

It's hard to tell from your letter if you're getting scooped a few weeks or a few months after meeting someone online, so I'm going to assume you're talking more than a few weeks, since you said you didn't want to get serious with anyone (well, not at first).

Here's the deal: Most people, women especially, do not want to end up in some perpetual email relationship. My guess is that whether you want to keep things strictly casual or not, you are not moving fast enough when it comes down to face-to-face contact. Maybe you're worried that the budding relationship will move too fast if you meet in person. Maybe you're more interested in a pen-pal-type arrangement than an actual relationship. Maybe you're just a bit slow getting out of the starting gate.

My concern is that you're being so cautious, you're taking yourself out of the dating pool entirely. You may think you're just keeping it casual and playing it safe, but women you communicate with will eventually expect to meet you. If you don't progress the relationship at a normal pace, they'll start to wonder why. And the reasons they'll come up with will be (1) you're not interested; (2) your wife has finally caught on; or (3) you're not the guy in your online photo.

You have two choices: You can either step up your game and be a bit more proactive, or, worst case scenario, if you really don't want to meet in person and you'd prefer to email and email and email, you can always tell women you're in prison. Sure, you'll eliminate a lot of candidates who want to steer clear of the felon crowd, but at least you won't have your email buddies clamoring to meet you. At least not for five to ten.

Best,

Lisa

Would You Date Brad Pitt, Tom Cruise, Paul Newman, Mel Gibson, or Ewan McGregor If You Met Them Online?

If you're like most women, you would have filtered them out, based on height, by checking the "5'10" or taller" box. There are a whole lot of nice, charming, and yes, short men out there, ladies. And sometimes tall, dark, and handsome ain't all it's cracked up to be. The greatest untapped dating resource in America is the short man. Be the first on your block to get one.

Seeing Past the Frog-Skin Jackets

We've all heard the saying "You can't judge a book by its cover," but when it comes to dating, we're all prone to snap judgments, right? We swoon over profiles of doctors and bankers the way we used to pore over details of TV heartthrobs and rock 'n' roll front men in the latest issue of *Teen Beat*.

But the man who wears socks with sandals or drips nacho cheese on his Mickey Mouse tie all night? He's a loser. My girl-friend Tina can weed through thirty profiles in about a minute and a half and filter out the guys she'd *never* go out with from the guys she'd *definitely* go out with. She's the Tomahawk missile of daters. And she's not alone.

Studies show we actually make a decision about whether or not we want to date someone within the first few minutes of meeting him.

And if "meeting him" is via an online dating profile, we likely spend even less time making a yay or nay decision.

But sometimes when we form our opinions of people too quickly, we may be missing out on someone great. Example? I recently received a letter from a single guy living with Mom and Dad who was having a hard time snagging a date.

Perception: He's a thirty-something leech. Dad's still paying the bills; Mom's still doing his laundry; and on alternate Friday nights, he gets to borrow the family station wagon.

Gee, I thought to myself after reading his first sentence, *how do I tell this guy that until he moves out of the basement, he's dooming himself to a social life comprised of microwave linguine and the all-you-can-rent plan at Blockbuster?*

Then I read the rest of his letter.

Reality: He's a successful guy, making $140K a year, who owns his own business (*and* his parents' home) and is living there to care for them because they suffer from health issues.

Screech. This guy just went from undateable loser to the best prospect on the planet in a single paragraph.

But most women weren't even getting to that.

The truth is, while we might be able to rely on our first impressions in person, they're hardly accurate when we're browsing profiles. Think about it. About 70 percent of all communication is nonverbal. When you meet people for the first time, you're not just making a judgment based on what they say but how they carry themselves, what they wear, how they smell, and how their chemistry reacts with yours. With a mere dating profile, you miss nearly all of that. So you base your judgments on things that feel important—but in the long run, they might not really matter. Like how tall someone is, what he does for a living, and, er, whether or not he still bunks at Mom and Dad's.

I advised him to lead with his strengths in his online profile: High income, professional, and business owner. I also suggested he change the language in his profile to reflect who he really was (without freaking out the women he might date). I told him to change how he framed up his living situation to more accurately reflect the truth: His parents live with him; he loves them and is responsible; and he is caring for them while they're ill. Soon, he had more dates. A lot more.

It's all about keeping your eyes open. A friend of mine met her future husband in a bar. He sat there nursing a beer, in a fashion-backward plaid shirt, and smiled at her all night. She, however, was quite busy making googly eyes at some other guy who, coincidentally, turned out to be married. At the end of the night (after discovering her first choice was not an option), she declared, "I think I'll give Plaid Guy a chance." She talked to him; they started dating, fell madly in love, and have been happily ever after ever since.

Her initial assessment, based on a one-minute conversation? Hardworking (good), reasonably handsome (could be better with a wardrobe makeover), police officer (too dangerous), with no handyman skills whatsoever (the horror!), and seeks long-term relationship. The real guy? Hardworking (good), goofy to her serious (fantastic), easygoing, sweet as pie, and worships the ground she walks on but doesn't take any of her crap. In other words, the exact perfect guy for her.

The thing that turned out to be magical in their relation-ship was that his personality was the perfect match for hers. While she could have brooded for days with a more closed-off partner, his lighthearted temperament was the perfect balance to hers. They shared similar financial, family, relationship, and educational values, which made them a great pair for a long-term relationship.

The lesson here? Sometimes there's a prince lurking beneath that frog-skin jacket. Try not to eliminate someone solely based on your snap reaction to their one-dimensional dating profile. If you dig just a little deeper, you might find exactly what you've been looking for in a most unexpected place.

Give Plaid Guy a chance.

What's Really Important?

When it comes to a happy relationship, five factors are strong indicators of how well the union will last:

1. Similar money management.

2. The ability of one or both partners to defuse tense situations or arguments (especially with humor or shared experiences), rather than digging in.

3. Compatible sex drives.

4. Willingness to talk through issues without stonewalling.

5. Mutual respect and regard, talking to each other without contempt.

Opposites Attract, But Do They Stick?

I am a social butterfly who has been known to exist for days on mini-quiches and cosmopolitans. I've voted for Democrats. I have a closet full of strappy stilettos. My husband, on the other hand, is a chemist. With an MBA. And a wardrobe that is comprised almost entirely of blue. On the surface, we're about as well matched as Carrie Bradshaw and Alex Trebek. On a deeper level, though, we're a perfect fit. We have the same views on money, family, and work. And perhaps more importantly, we both like movie trivia and Cherry Garcia.

Frankly, I believe that there's a reason opposites attract. It's because, sometimes, you *can* have too much of a good thing. There can be problems with dating someone who is exactly like you, especially if you end up together for the long haul. Take two driven, career-addicted, type A, clawing-to-get-to-the-top types. Sure, they'll have a lot in common. They'll understand each others' schedules, negotiation issues, and endless business travel. But say they get married. In this relocation-for-promotion business climate, eventually somebody would have to put his or her career path in jeopardy. And the thing that once brought them together would either force one of them to change or tear them apart.

Two passionate hotheads might be crazy for each other in the start of a relationship, but eventually all the makeup sex in the world isn't going to smooth over the hurt feelings from dramatic door slamming, screaming matches, and conclusion-jumping. Wouldn't a hot-tempered person be a better match with someone who had the ability to stay calm when the feathers hit the ceiling fan?

Maybe we just need to look at what we think of as our "opposite." Frequently, the traits we're looking for in a mate are not the traits that would be most compatible with what we really want in the long run. A career-driven girlfriend of mine, like many women in her position, only dates men who are similarly successful in business. Why? She doesn't want to marry "down."

I wonder sometimes if she widened her pool of eligibles just a bit, she might just meet Mr. Right.

For example, she's highly competitive but tends to argue with her partners, because she chooses men who are as competitive as she is. The problem with a relationship where two people always need to win an argument is that, eventually, somebody has to lose. She might have more peaceful relationships with someone who has better compromising skills.

She's a woman who can take care of herself and tends to date similarly oriented men. But she might feel more nurtured in a relationship with someone who is more of a caretaker. Think of it this way: Who's going to be a better fit for someone who travels four days a week for work? A person who is cranky and exhausted from traveling four days a week himself? Or someone with a lower-pressure job who can manage the home front (especially helpful if she has children or pets) and run a bath for her when she drags her suitcase into the foyer at three in the morning?

Relationships tend to work more harmoniously when there's a flower and a gardener, a rock star and a manager, a yin and a yang.

Sometimes we have such a clear picture in our heads of what we're looking for that we miss someone even better. It's a good idea to remember that a person, unlike a movie or a trashy beach novel, can't be summed up in a quick review. A mountain climber and a concert violinist may appear to be completely different on the surface, but maybe they have similar families, belong to the same new-age church, and are both addicted to sushi. Maybe they're not so opposite after all.

So can opposites really make it for the long haul? Yes. And no. Basically, what makes love work boils down to our similarities, not our differences. As you're writing your online profile, pay attention to see if what you're looking for matches how you see yourself. Then, if you're feeling really brave, do a search for someone who is your complete opposite. You might just find your perfect match.

Grown-Up Dating Fact

Despite having major doubts before the first date, most singles are sure of one thing: 85 percent say they know before the end of a first date if they'll be interested in getting to know someone better. Think that's fast? Thirty percent say they know within the first five minutes. Men (7 percent) were twice as likely as women (3.4 percent) to say they can measure their future interest in someone at first sight. This is why it's really important to check your teeth for stray chunks of broccoli *before* you open the door.

Source: Colgate Simply White Dating Survey

When to Cut Your Losses

Most people email for about three weeks before initiating a personal meeting. If it's been more than two months and you haven't met yet, odds are you never will. (And there's usually a good reason for that: maybe your online sweetie is married, confined to his rec room wearing one of those prison-issue ankle bracelets, or is, hmm, otherwise unavailable.) Unless you're just looking for a pen pal, you might want to chalk this one up to experience and move on.

If You Can't Be With the One You Love, Honey, Love the One You're With

Last, remember online dating (and dating in general) should be fun. Don't think of it as a tedious interview process for your next spouse. Think of dating as a way to connect with other people, have a little fun, and maybe learn something new. Dating is a pastime that should be enjoyed and savored. Practice your flirting skills, have fun, and don't worry about where the relationship is going. Whether you end up with a new friend or a new love, concentrate on the journey, not the destination.

So the next time you're man shopping at three in the morning, see if you can gain a greater insight from the pixels he's posted. Upon further examination, you might learn he has a collection of classic movies on his mantle, drinks Rolling Rock out of the bottle, and seems to *really* enjoy Italian food, judging by the cute little manicotti smudge on his chin.

The All-New Dating Game: Team Dating

Want more fun online dates, with less lying and better safety? Try team dating, the latest and greatest in online dating. Instead of the usual hookup for two, team daters date in, well, teams. Three of my closest pals set up a group date with three of yours. Here's why I think the idea of team dating is a fabulous idea.

Safety in Numbers

Instead of meeting a complete stranger for drink all alone, you'll meet a throng of complete strangers, accompanied by your closest friends. Plus, there are no worries about driving home alone—you know your pals will make certain you get home safely.

No Online "Faux"tos

Your date's friends will keep him honest. He's far less likely to post a photo of himself when he was twenty pounds lighter with significantly more hair and fewer wrinkles if he knows that his friends (and yours!) will call him on it at the moment of truth, when you all meet up for the first time. The threat of public humiliation is a fine tool to keep us all walking the straight line.

To Tell the Truth

You've probably experienced the lying that is rampant in online dating. The great thing about dating someone in front of his friends? It keeps him honest. No remaking his two-year stint as a seventh-grade ball boy for the Hickory Crawdads into a near-miss career as a major-league pitcher (if only it hadn't been for that damned knee injury!). No glossing over that seven-year employment gap as a period of reflection to write a novel/live with Buddhist monks/join the Peace Corps, if it was really just chronic laziness in the form of one bad pizza-flipping gig after another.

Why Is This Catching On?

Frankly, it's way more fun than regular online dating. If your date turns out to be a dud, you'll can still have a fabulous time hanging out with your friends. Plus, you won't have to worry about dishing the details of your date-gone-wrong the next day over coffee or margaritas; your closest pals will be there to witness the crash and burn firsthand. Plus, as we've discussed, team dating eliminates most of the concerns that crop up in regular online dating: safety and honesty.

While some sites are suggesting daters register as teams, I think this is where the concept falls apart. Say you pick out a cutie online; then you have to talk your team into dating the rest of his or her team. The chances of the eight of you matching up like sweater sets from Talbots is pretty damned slim.

So how do you partake in team dating without forcing your dearest friends into a triple-wingwoman formation? You and three of your girlfriends pick out your own dates online and meet up at a single location, say, the bowling alley or a local watering hole.

At worst, your date will be a social experiment gone wrong. At best, you and your teammates may find you've all hit a home run.

Now, *that's* major-league dating.

Letters to Lisa ♥♥♥♥♥♥♥♥

Dear Lisa,

I have a dating dilemma. I have been using an online dating service and have met many nice guys. These men will take me out the first time and say that they don't want to date anyone else or take their name off the site after meeting me. How can I let them know that they aren't the only one I am dating? I feel I need to be honest with them, but I also don't want to reveal my personal business to them either.

Dating Dilemma

Dear Dating Dilemma,

First, let me commend you for not jumping into an exclusive relationship with someone you've dated only once. Good for you!

Second, remember that if your guy friends choose to stop dating other women the second they meet you, well, that's really fabulous.

However, you are under no obligation to do the same. Don't feel you must confess your dating habits to someone you barely know. Your other dates are your own private business. You can maintain your honesty by telling the truth if they ask you if you're seeing other people and by being perfectly honest (either way) if they ask for exclusivity. If your answer is yes, then ditch the other guys; if it's no or not yet, simply say you're just not quite ready to take things to that level yet.

Kisses,

Lisa

Chapter 8

Liars, Criminals, and the Freak Next Door

Dating can be fraught with disaster, from pathological liars to guys who send you porn in their first email contact, all the way to con artists who scheme to set up credit-card scams right from your bedroom. Below you'll find some helpful advice to protect your heart, your mind, and your bank account.

Liar, Liar, Profile's on Fire

Almost everybody lies. We tell Aunt Edna that we'd *love* to come to her nursing home's four-hour musical production of *The Best Little Whorehouse in Texas* on Thursday night, but our boss is making us work late. We call ourselves "athletic," when the only sports we actively participate in occur via television broadcast, riding a Barcalounger while balancing a plate of jalapeno nachos. And sometimes we prune just enough birthdays off our age to bump us down to the next lowest age bracket.

A recent study on Internet dating found that online daters claimed to be richer, better educated, taller, thinner, and more likely to have blonde hair than the rest of the population. Uh huh.

Dr. Marianne Dainton, a communication professor at La Salle University, says, "Up to 62 percent of statements made in conversation could be classified as deceptive. Do the math: That means that only 38 percent of statements in our everyday conversations are purely truthful."

Gregory Hartley, former military interrogator and co-author of the I-couldn't-put-it-down book called *How to Spot a Liar: Why People Don't Tell the Truth . . . and How You Can Catch Them,* says, "We live in a society that values wealth and beauty. Most people are not willing to just be an average person. When we meet in person we have our looks, our fashion sense, our sense of humor, and even body chemistry working for us. When we walk into a room, potential partners quickly assess our value within minutes (if not seconds). Most of us have learned how to manage the trappings of that game. Now in a virtual dating environment, where everyone is beautiful, wealthy, educated, and athletic, who would not want to exaggerate to stand out in the crowd?

"We are working in an area that is new to most people. The world's oldest game on the world's newest field. We are constantly striving to improve our technique. The Internet dating scene is about filtering among the vast numbers for an opportunity: *If I stand out, I get the first chance.* It is about evolution. It is as-primitive-as-we-get meets as-modern-as-we-get."

But what's the harm of a few white lies in a new online dating relationship? Who does it really hurt to add a few inches or subtract a few pounds? Or marriages? Or felonies?

Hartley says, "This depends on the lie; sure, we all omit facts about our past. I am no advocate of radical truth. Do you really want someone to come out and tell you how many people they have slept with? Or tell you how badly you suck at your favorite hobby?"

There are basically two types of lies: lies by *omission* (allowing someone to believe something that isn't true) and lies of *commission* (telling someone an outright lie.)

Both experts agree that lying by commission is considered worse. Hartley warns, "In my mind, a lie at the beginning of a relationship is asking for trouble later. No lie can stand alone. Your life is like a photo album. Lies (typically not well thought out) are more like a snapshot and lack detail to relate to the rest of the album. To sustain a lie, you must tell other lies. Before you know it, deception is rampant."

Which means those harmless little white lies are more harmful than we thought. Can pretending to be something you're *not quite* keep you from finding a real relationship? If you are one of two people offering up their fake selves, how can you possibly meet your true soul mate?

You can't. Instead of connecting with someone who appreciates you as a total hottie/*Love Boat*–trivia savant/gourmet-popcorn aficionado, you doom yourself to disappointing all the people you meet. As great as you are, you're not what they expected. And the reason is that you led them to expect something else.

Hartley says, "People are composed of many roles. All of these roles contribute to the whole person. It is very easy to become enamored of a role that you observe. Some of these roles come from the entertainment industry, others from co-workers, friends, and family. The problem is that even the role you are so eager to recreate is only one aspect of the person you are envious of."

But why do we lie in the first place? Fear. Fear we're not good enough. Fear we'll be found out. Fear we won't be loved for who we are. Fear we'll be left. Which is why we have to ask ourselves, do we really want to be with someone who wouldn't love us if we were fifteen pounds heavier with brown hair?

Hartley sums it up: "You bait the trap and catch your quarry, only to discover you have no place to accommodate the beast."

So the next time you're wavering about whether you should pad the ol' profile, just remember you're not making yourself more likely to find the man of your dreams, but less.

And that's no lie.

Letters to Lisa   ❤❤❤❤❤❤❤

Dear Lisa,

I have been chatting (as friends) online for over year with a notorious NBA player who lives near me and is married. We haven't met in person, but I went to one of his games, and he noticed me. He called me one time and confessed he'd driven by my house. He's a Bible thumper, follows the Bible literally, and says he's happy with his marriage. The last thing I want to be is a home wrecker.

He pushes away from me, because he thinks he's getting too close. He ignored me for weeks and then popped back into my life. I absolutely agree with his protocol, but I find myself already in love with him. I am obsessed with him. He's playing with my emotions and says he can't stop thinking about me. He says he would meet me face-to-face, but he's afraid we might hook up. I don't know what to do. I really like him and always wonder if I have a chance.

Bouncing Around

Dear Bouncing,

This guy is an E! True Hollywood Story *just waiting to happen.*

That is, assuming he's the real deal and not some thirteen-year-old kid yanking your chain from his basement in Dubuque, Iowa.

You asked me if I think you have a chance. You have a chance, all right: the chance to become the next Monica Lewinsky.

Sweetie, if there's a Mrs., he's Mr. Wrong. You said yourself that you don't want to be a home wrecker, so don't. Nothing good can come of dating a married man. Even if he left his wife (he won't) and married you (he won't), your relationship with him would have less than a 5 percent chance of surviving just one year (after which he would likely get right back into his old patterns and start screwing around on you).

Not to mention the two of you would be responsible for screwing up the lives of at least three people—more if kids are involved.

You may agree with his protocol, but I think it sucks. If he's married, he shouldn't be flirting with women in chat rooms. He shouldn't be calling the women he meets in chat rooms. And he most certainly should not be doing late-night drive-bys.

Here's my advice to you: Cut off all contact with him immediately.

As far as the Bible thumping goes, I'm pretty sure there's more than one passage in the good book about being faithful and honorable to your wife. Maybe he has a different version than the one I'm familiar with, but the book he's thumping sounds more like one you might pick up in a convenience store in a plain brown wrapper.

Best,

Lisa

Online Dating Deal Breakers

While you're learning how to weed out undesirables, it's important to consider how you come across over the wires. Let's take a look at a few point-and-click tactics that can give eligibles the wrong idea. These tips can also help in reverse—if you see someone using them, it's probably best to steer clear.

Deal Breaker: Spray and Pray

Men tend to use this particular method more than women do, but I'm sure there are probably a few offenders in the female sex as well. The Spray and Pray is when a person sends out a whole bunch of nonspecific, impersonal emails (the Spray) and then keeps their fingers crossed that somebody will take the bait and respond (the Pray). Most of us would like to feel special and know that someone is interested in us personally, rather than just being the target of a massive direct-mail love campaign. The fix: Check out the profiles of people you're actually interested in, and email or IM them with a personal note.

Deal Breaker: Searching for Veterinarian Ken

This tactic involves being so specific in your profile you come off as shallow and overly picky. Searching for a six-foot, forty-four-year-old blonde vet with no kids and a six-figure income? Instead of zeroing in on the person you've been dreaming of, you may be pushing him away by appearing completely superficial. Remember, your profile is a wish list; it's not an order form. The last thing you want to do is give the impression you're filling out an application for a mail-order groom. Put the things that are truly important to you (religion, education, etc.), and leave the specifics (job, eye color, pets' names, etc.) to chance.

Deal Breaker: No Boundaries

One of the biggest blunders is asking inappropriate or overly personal questions in an early email or telephone chat, such as "Do you have any pictures of yourself in a Speedo?" or "How much money do you make?" Another no-no: sending unrequested pictures of yourself in a towel or naked. Instead of having the desired effect, you may just leave the recipient wondering, *Why does she have naked pictures of herself lying around, and who else has she sent them to?*

Deal Breaker: Eternal Emailer

Don't let online dating replace actual romance. Online dating is a fantastic way to meet people, but make sure your intentions are clear if you'd like to email eternally and never, ever go on a date. Most people expect to meet eventually if there's a connection. Many singles believe that if an in-person meeting doesn't take place, something's amiss: *Is she married? Doing time for bank fraud?* Maybe typing into a computer screen for a couple hours a day is enough of a relationship for you, but for most people, it's a bust.

Deal Breaker: Out of the Ballpark

The final deal breaker is emailing someone when you're WAY outside his criteria. He's looking for a thirty-something, college-educated Christian who wants marriage, and you're a fifty-ish party-girl atheist who didn't survive community college? Even if he does look fabulous in his photo, it's impolite to completely disregard his desire to meet someone he feels compatible with. Obviously, it's probably okay to go ahead and make contact if you're just slightly out of range (maybe you're five-foot-ten rather than five-foot-eight), but be sure to say so up front and respect his wishes if he chooses to stick to his original criteria. Nobody is right for everyone, but everyone's right for someone.

Letters to Lisa ♥♥♥♥♥♥♥♥

Dear Lisa,

I know what your stand is on dating married men—I feel the same way. But what about men who are not with their exes anymore? He hasn't been with her for a long time, but they haven't officially gotten the divorce yet (but they are definitely divorced in their hearts). I don't sleep with him, but we love each other a lot. I would like him to be "the one." He always said that after his marriage broke up, he wouldn't marry again, but he seems to talk a lot about marrying me. I believe he really wants to marry me—he talks about popping the question and he recently said he knows that this year he has to get a divorce. (Money is what stops him.)

I want to do the right thing and either kick it up or eliminate him as a potential husband. He always expresses his fear that someone else is going to scoop me up if he doesn't act. Can you please help me?

Hopeful Bride

Dear Hopeful,

I hate to break this to you, but there's not a state in the Union that considers being "divorced in their hearts" anything close to actually being divorced. In fact, being divorced in your heart is exactly the same thing as being married. Exactly.

I think you should be running from this man as quickly as possible. Why? First, he can't marry you; he's already married, and from what it looks like to me, this isn't going to be changing anytime soon. Second, you say that he talks about marrying you and expresses a *fear that someone else will scoop you up if he doesn't act, but guess what? He doesn't act. Last, if you hit that million-to-one shot and he does get off his $#%$, get a divorce, and marry you, I'm sure you'd be spending your entire marriage wondering when he'll be telling his NEW girlfriend that you and he are "divorced in your hearts."*

Dump him.

Lisa

E-Dumping

He writes eleven-page emails about his hamster, Mr. Beekins, or won't stop talking about his fetish for nursing shoes. Whatever the reason, it's just not working out.

And while online dating makes meeting your perfect match easier than ever, it can also make rejection more casual. In its very early stages, online dating sometimes feels more like the romantic equivalent of shopping the Lands' End catalog (*A comfortable, stylish classic—perfect for a night at the movies or lounging with friends. Machine washable, lay flat to dry.*) than actually interacting with a thinking, feeling human being.

And if you've never actually met for a date, are you actually dumping him? Or are you just not pursuing a relationship?

Say you've exchanged a few emails and feel certain he is not "the one." What next?

Most people just stop emailing, which can lead to confusion on the part of the dumpee. Are you dead? The newest contestant on *Survivor*? Trapped in a well? Certainly the strategy will work—eventually they'll stop emailing you and just go away—but a nicer, more courteous strategy is to drop them a quick email that says, "It's been nice meeting you, but I don't see it going any further." Then thank them, wish them well, and be on your way.

If you're not interested when a man contacts you initially, a "rejection template" is an effective way to say thanks, but no thanks. If you've had a few email contacts already, then a short, personal note is best.

Rejection Template—The Initial Contact

Dear _____,

Thanks for taking the time to contact me. I'm very flattered by your interest but don't believe we'd be a good fit.

Best of luck!

YOUR NAME HERE

Letters to Lisa

Hi Lisa,

I am a woman who just got dumped.

Why, when I knew my mate had found someone new, wouldn't he admit it? I confronted my ex with my suspicions and, of course, he denied it. There were no harsh words, tears, or yelling during our talk—it was just me letting him know that I was aware of what was going on and that in order for me to put closure on our relationship, I needed to hear the truth from him. No go. He wouldn't budge.

He left a few weeks ago without so much as a good-bye, which confirmed my suspicions but brought me no closure. Since then, I have read many online forums on the subject of breaking up and cheating, and it seems that almost every one stated that while people may have cheated, they almost always owned up to it. Why couldn't/wouldn't my ex do that for me? I told him I'd let him go—I just wanted his honesty. How much easier could I have made it for him?

Sincerely,

In the Dumps

Dear Dumps,

First off, I'm so sorry for what happened to you. I know it hurts. I'm not sure what you've been reading, but I can tell you with certainty that it is a rarity that people will own up to cheating, even if faced with a smoking gun. (Or smoking bed sheets.)

Here's why your ex wouldn't admit to it: It was wrong; he knows it; and he doesn't want to deal with an unpleasant situation. This is also why some men will just end a relationship by never calling again. They don't want to face a nasty breakup scene, so they just avoid the situation altogether.

I do understand your need for closure, but unfortunately, I just don't think you're going to get it from him. What you need is confirmation that your suspicions were real, that you weren't crazy or imagining things. He's not going to tell you what you need to hear, so I will. You should trust your gut. If you think he was cheating on you, you're right. (According to private investigators, cheating IS occurring in more than 90 percent of relationships where it is suspected.) We women frequently doubt our instincts, even when every bone in our bodies is screaming a truth. Believe in yourself; you are right. Don't look to him for closure—look to yourself.

Best,

Lisa

But what happens when the relationship is more serious than a few friendly emails? One of the advantages of online dating is the ability to meet people all over the world. When you're talking cross-continental dating, sometimes IMs and cybersex are the permanent reality of your relationship. So what's the best policy when it comes to ending a three-month- or year-long online romance?

Obviously, you don't want to hurt someone who has developed feelings for you—or worse, maybe it's clear you're dealing with a nut, and you don't want to be the trigger for an economy-sized bottle of Prozac and a six-week stint at the Bendy Willow Psychiatric Center.

When it comes to actual relationships, online or offline, there are two important things to remember: first, be nice. After all, what goes around comes around. You're probably not going to be on the receiving end of "happily ever after" if you go around torturing your exes for sport.

Second, be sure to make your reasons relevant only to you. In other words, it's not him; it's you. Say, "This isn't working for me." Stick with your basis and keep repeating yourself over and over if necessary. It's impossible for someone to argue with you about reasons that pertain only to you. If you end up getting sucked into a situation where you have to list grounds for wanting it to be over, you may find yourself in for an encore. If you say, "You're too insecure," or "We fight all the time," your partner may offer to change, taking all the air out of your breakup and landing you right back in the relationship.

Rejection Template—For Someone You've Had a Few Emails or Phone Contacts With

Dear _____,

It's been so interesting* to meet you, but I don't see this going any further. I truly appreciate your understanding, and I wish you all the best!

Sincerely,

YOUR NAME HERE

The word "interesting" covers a wide variety of flaws, and is a kinder substitute for "boring," "bizarre," "mind-numbing," or "unbelievably unpleasant."

Letters to Lisa

Dear Lisa,

I met this amazing man two months ago. We're from two different cities, so we have been emailing back and forth to each other. He came across as so sincere, sensitive, and sweet. I have never met a man like him.

So about three weeks ago, he decided to drive up to see me. Seeing him was just too much. We were so connected, and it was out of this world. We both fell in love. After he'd gone back, he emailed me like usual, and I did the same. And then, something strange happened: he left a beautiful, loving voicemail for me over three weeks ago, and I left another voicemail for him two days later—and that was it! I never heard back from him.

Please, did he just take an easy way out? Why didn't he even call or email to "break up" with me?

Missing in Action

Dear Missing,

Let me start out by saying that there are just some men in life that appear to drop off the face of the earth a few days after you have a fabulously amazing time together. Do they develop amnesia? Get hit by runaway tour buses? Get snatched by aliens or multilevel marketers for medical experiments and routine brainwashing? Who knows? Don't beat yourself up about it—it just happens.

In your case, however, something seems a little strange. Something in my gut is telling me there's something a little fishy with this guy— maybe a girlfriend. It's possible that the sudden stop in communication has happened because he (1) suddenly felt guilty, or (2) he was discovered, and he's busy getting himself out of the doghouse with chick number one.

Either way, I'd put him out of your mind until he contacts you and it's clear his amnesia has been miraculously cured and he's not otherwise involved. As for why he didn't call to break up with you—the reason is simple. Any breakup is bound to be an uncomfortable situation, and many men will try to avoid what they perceive will be a long, drawn-out, talk-it-to-death tear fest.

Kisses,

Lisa

Strangers in the Night

What if you're pretty certain that the person on the other end of the net is not a liar, freak, or criminal? Well, it's important to remember that while you may *feel* a real connection with someone you meet online, that person is still a stranger. Be sure to keep your personal information private (such as your home address and phone number). There are a number of online-dating scams that target women over forty. Don't lend your date money; don't get engaged to someone you haven't met in person; don't accept packages at your home for someone you've been dating online (this is a scam that involves Internet theft of credit card numbers and having the stolen goods sent to the home of the unsuspecting "girlfriend"). If something feels not quite right, listen to your gut. You wouldn't leave your tax return in the middle of the parking lot at the Bowl-a-Rama, so be careful to protect yourself when you're dating online as well.

I'll Be There

Make sure that when you meet your date in the real world for the first few times (at least), you drive yourself to and from your meeting place, carry a cell phone with you, and tell a friend exactly where you're going, with whom, and when you'll be home. Agree you'll call your pal the minute you get home. Make sure the meeting place is on your turf—in a restaurant that you know, in a neighborhood where you're comfortable. If you ever feel uncomfortable, cut the date short and leave. Don't let your online date pick you up at home until you know each other *in person* a lot better.

Getting Down, Out of Town

Online dating has created a unique situation in that it's now just as easy to fall for someone two cities away or across the globe as it is to fall for the man next door. But meeting an online date in person out of town poses some special safety concerns. First, use the same safety guidelines you would for an offline date in your own city. Second, stay in a hotel; never EVER stay with someone you don't actually know. (And if you can't afford to stay in a hotel, skip the trip for now.) Keep your hotel location (or at least your room number) private (just as you would your home address), and get to and from the date (and your hotel) via your own transportation—either a rental car or a taxi. As romantic as it might seem to have your date pick you up from the airport, it is especially important to take safety precautions when you are out of town. Finally, as tempting as it may be to spend a week with your new online romance, remember that chemistry: Keep your first trip short and sweet (two days max) until you're positive there's a real connection in person.

Letters to Lisa   ♥♥♥♥♥♥♥♥

Dear Lisa,

I have two questions for you. I have been talking to a few guys online. I know you say that a man should always pick you up at your front door, but I do feel that this is a different situation. Wouldn't it be safer to meet them in a public area? I have been in contact with them for a little while, and to be honest, I don't feel threatened—but the fact is that you never know these days.

Also, you say that we should never call a guy back. If a guy calls me and leaves me a message and I don't call him back, won't he just assume I'm not interested in him and never call me again? I mean, I know if I call a guy and he doesn't call me back, I never call again.

Thanks,

Modern Love

Dear Modern,

You sound like a fabulous woman, and I'm delighted to see you taking charge of your love life.

You're right. While I do think a man should always pick you up for a date in a more traditional dating setting (friend of a friend, a guy you met at work, etc.), when meeting someone you've met online for the first several times, you should not only meet them in a public place but also follow a few other safety rules.

As for whether or not you need to return a guy's calls, here's the skinny: It doesn't matter what you would do if a guy didn't call you back, because you are not a guy. You're a woman.

If we call a man and he doesn't call us back right away, we start analyzing every nuance of every movement, flirtation, and conversation, and dissecting it for clues:

"Gee, I really liked him, and I thought he liked me. But maybe he didn't. But if he likes me, he'll call by Tuesday. Okay, Wednesday. Okay, I'll give him until Friday. But maybe he was just being nice, and he doesn't really want to go out with me. Maybe he already has a girlfriend, or maybe he just got out of a bad relationship. He did look at me kind of funny when I ordered a Pink Lady at the bar—maybe he thinks I'm not uptown enough for him. But he ordered

beer! Maybe he thinks I'm too uptown. Or maybe he's on an out-of-town business trip to Belize, and he hasn't even picked up my message . . ."

And a man thinks,

"She's not home. I'll try later."

Lisa

Dating 911: What to Do If Your Date Goes Bad

Most women have fairly safe experiences with online dating, but it's important to always be on your guard.

If you ever feel uncomfortable on a date, trust your instincts, and do whatever you can to keep yourself safe. Many women who have found themselves in dangerous situations had a gut feeling that something was amiss but ignored it anyway.

Make sure that you always carry a cell phone with you and that it is charged. If you are walking to your car, tell the restaurant manager that you feel unsafe, and ask him or her to have someone walk you to your car.

If no one is available to escort you, hit 9-1-1 on your phone and keep your finger on the "send" button. That way, if trouble happens, you'll have one quick button to push, rather than fumbling around for four.

If your date surprises you and pressures you to get in a car with him when your instincts tell you not to, do everything you can to avoid getting in the car. Remember, being out in public is safer than being alone in a car with a stranger.

Finally, it's always a good idea for women to work a few self-defense classes into the ol' workout schedule.

Part 2

Get Lucky

Chapter 9

Is He Just Dating You for Sex? (And Is That a Bad Thing?)

Boom Boom Boomers

A recent study by Wanobe.com says more than one-third (37 percent) of baby boomers are willing to sleep with someone on the first date, which is twice the number of Generation Xers (just 18 percent of the under-forty crowd) that would do so.

But before you start buying your condoms in bulk, you should know that all that easy action comes with a price: Of the women who said they'd be willing to go for it on the first night, 76 percent said they'd only do so if a man took them to dinner first and picked up the tab.

That's right, folks: The keys to the kingdom can be had for a nice bottle of wine, a slab of beef, and a blooming onion.

"Tramp" Is in the Eye of the Beholder

Most experts believe that women over forty are more open to sex because they grew up in an era of free love, sexual freedom, swingers, feminism, and the introduction of the birth control pill.

Generation Xers, on the other hand, grew up in an era of AIDS, herpes, single mothers, date-rape drugs, and media coverage of child molesters.

Radio host Kidder Kaper says, "The simple truth is that for boomers, sex was presented as liberating, and for Xers, sex was dangerous."

Add to that the fact that most women over forty are no longer looking for someone to start a family with or provide for them financially. In many cases, we're just looking for companionship and fun. And if you're not in the market for someone you can spend the rest of your life with, you have a lot more options.

> **"This is probably the only time in my life when I would consider sleeping with a Denzel Washington look-alike who's dumb as a rock. You can always kick him out before breakfast."**
> **—Linda**

The Bad News? He Thinks You're Easy. The Good News? You Don't Care.

Reputation, schmeputation.

Once women begin to hit forty, we're not particularly worried about what our friends might think of our bedroom antics. We're comfortable enough in our own skin to live without fear of disapproval.

As one over-forty woman, Susan, says, "Sometimes you just want sex."

Does "Free Love" Come at a Price?

Diseases. Misunderstandings. Thirty-seven-hour pharmaceutical erections.

A recent AARP study found that 45 percent of men and 38 percent of women between the ages of forty and fifty-nine have sex once a week.

No-strings sex can seem wild and romantic, but the morning-after (and week-after) implications can suck the fun out of even the wildest night of lovemaking.

Because pregnancy is no longer an issue, many women over forty are forgoing condoms altogether. Sometimes skipping the condom is a matter of practicality: Many men, as they age, have more difficulty maintaining an erection.

The AARP study also found that 76 percent of singles forty-five and older don't use protection when having sex.

But skipping the protection can be dangerous.

Grown-Up Dating Fact

According to the National Institutes of Health (NIH), both men and women may find that it takes longer to become aroused as they grow older. This may be caused by a variety of issues, including health problems, medications, or stress.

Unfortunately, there are a whole new host of sexually transmitted diseases (STDs) that were not a factor during the last sexual revolution, and sometimes condoms offer the only protection. Forty years ago, most STDs were curable with a shot of penicillin. Now, unprotected sex can kill you.

The Centers for Disease Control (CDC) reports shocking increases in STD transmission for those over forty-five, especially in women. In fact, the CDC reports that people in their forties contract STDs at double the rate of people in their twenties.

According to the CDC, chlamydia is the most commonly reported infectious disease in the United States, followed by gonorrhea, which is increasingly resistant to drugs.

The number of new HIV infections among older women is increasing quickly as well: Between 1998 and 2000, AIDS cases nearly doubled among women fifty and older—from 8.9 percent to 15 percent. *U.S. Pharmacist* reported that "in the U.S., approximately 10 percent of AIDS cases occur in patients fifty or older, and 3 percent of all AIDS cases occur in patients over age sixty. Data regarding new AIDS cases from 1990 to 1992 indicated a decrease in incidence among persons thirty or younger, while an increase of 17 percent was seen in those sixty or older."

The Lowdown on Troubles Down Below

Chlamydia

Chlamydia is a bacterial infection that can easily be cured with antibiotics, but it is usually asymptomatic and often undiagnosed. Untreated, it can cause severe health consequences for women, including pelvic inflammatory disease (PID), ectopic pregnancy, and infertility. Up to 40 percent of females with untreated chlamydia infections develop PID. In addition, women infected with chlamydia are up to five times more likely to become infected with HIV, if exposed.

Gonorrhea

While gonorrhea is easily cured, untreated cases can lead to serious health problems. Among women, gonorrhea is a major cause of PID, which can lead to chronic pelvic pain, ectopic pregnancy, and infertility. Studies suggest that presence of gonorrhea infection makes an individual three to five times more likely to acquire HIV, if exposed.

Source: Centers for Disease Control.

Letters to Lisa ♥♥♥♥♥♥♥♥

Dear Lisa,

I just met a great guy. He's intelligent, sexy, and classy.

We had lunch last Sunday, and it ended up lasting for about seven hours. During our lunch, he showed me some modeling pictures that he had taken earlier. He also showed me two photocopied images of himself naked, because he said he knew I'd be comfortable with them. He said that they were pictures that were taken by his girlfriend, even though the pictures looked professionally taken. Later that night as we were making out, he pulled out his unit, which looked to be about ten inches long and very thick. How can I tell if he's had a penile implant?

I am afraid that all he wants from me is sex. I noticed a condom in his pocket on our date. How do I keep from getting sexual with men on the first date? This has already cost me men in the past.

I am tired of the pump-and-dump lifestyle, so please help me stop acting like a slut. I am a good person, but for some reason, when I am attracted to a guy, I always get frisky too soon. When should I get intimate with a guy? Is it possible to build a lasting relationship with someone that I sleep with by the second date?

Thanks,

Pump and Dump

Dear Pump and Dump,

Sweetie, I don't even know where to start with this one.

You begin by saying he's sexy and classy, and just two sentences later, he's showing you naked pictures of himself (during lunch, no less). I'm guessing you're basing your sexy/classy observation on something other than that creepy move.

Is it possible to build a lasting relationship with someone you sleep with on the second date? Sure, but it's not very likely. As unfair as it may be, most guys don't want to be with a woman they perceive to be easy. True, it's an unfair double standard (after all, he's doing it, too), but it is a reality. The other drawback to sleeping with a man too soon is that we women tend to get emotionally attached to someone we're having sex with much more quickly. Give yourself a little time to get to know and evaluate a guy to see if he's actually someone you're interested in being with, before post-sex bliss makes your judgment hazy.

Clearly, you're not happy with what you call the "pump and dump." So how can you keep from hopping into bed right away? Well, for starters, try to wait at least a month before you start sleeping with a guy. If you're having trouble controlling your desire, you'll need a fallback plan. Here it is: wear your ugliest, rattiest, granny panties on your date. You know the ones I'm talking about—the ones you wear when you haven't done laundry for two weeks. If you need extra reinforcement, don't shave your legs. Or your armpits. There is no greater motivator for a woman to keep her clothes on than prickly legs and the possible exposure of revolting underwear.

To answer your concern about whether or not your classy guy has had himself surgically enhanced, I consulted an expert in the field of penile surgery. Dr. Gary Alter, a Beverly Hills plastic surgeon and assistant clinical professor of plastic surgery at UCLA, says that a surgically enlarged penis may look somewhat irregular (like being ten inches long, for instance) and may feel lumpy or firm in certain areas if the girth has been enlarged. Depending on the technique used, the enhanced gentleman may have a scar in the pubic area or at the end of the penis.

If you're truly looking for a lasting relationship, set your standards a little higher, and remember that you are a fabulous, unique, amazing woman deserving of love. Which means you don't call yourself a slut. You don't sleep with men you barely know. And you don't accept a second date from someone who whips out naked photos on the first date.

Kisses,

Lisa

Talk Dirty to Your Doctor

One of the biggest health problems women over forty face is that their doctors stop asking them about their sex lives. Maybe doc doesn't want to hear about the bedroom antics of anybody over twenty-four; maybe it's out of respect; or maybe they think you stop having sex once you're past your prime childbearing years. The problem is, if they don't ask, they may not spot problems as they occur, and you could be missing out on important information vital to your health.

I know it can feel weird to confess to your doctor that you're sexually active, but it's important. Do it anyway.

Feelings, Nothing More than Feelings

While the beat of the sexual revolution goes on, sometimes there are still hurt feelings in the morning. You may go into a sexual encounter thinking you just want sex and find yourself emotionally attached once the deed is done. This is because oxytocin, a feel-good bonding chemical, is released in a woman's brain during sex.

So, it's important to give some thought to what you want (and don't want) before the clothes hit the floor. Make sure you do a gut check (not the kind where you see if your belly pooch is visible under your nightgown—the other kind) to figure out what you're looking for going in—sex, friendship, or a long-term committed relationship—and have some assurances that you and your partner are on the same page.

The (Good and Bad) Tricks of Old Age

Why Is It Taking So Long?

Many women find that as we age, it takes a heck of a lot longer to get turned on than it used to. Give yourself a break. It's natural for our sexual responses to slow down as we get older; what's most important is that you enjoy the experience. (See Chapter 10 for tips on how to do just that!)

Late Bloomers

Maybe you got married young; maybe you never had a chance to express your sexuality; or maybe forty (or fifty or sixty) hit, and you don't give a crap anymore. Many women experience a sort of sexual revolution of their own once they leave a marriage and find themselves, through some miracle of sex toys or a fortuitous pairing with an adventurous partner. Sometimes you find you've been suppressing your sexual urges your whole life. Sometimes you didn't even realize they were ever there.

If you hit this stage, you may not only want to experiment with a number and variety of partners but try out the trapeze section at the adult-entertainment store as well. Go ahead—just be sure to protect yourself.

Viagra: Friend or Foe?

Dr. Myra Belgeri, associate professor at the St. Louis College of Pharmacy, provided answers to the most commonly asked questions about Viagra and similar ED treatments. (Yes, ladies, I red-faced it, so you don't have to.)

When should you use it? It really depends if chronic conditions are controlled—ED can be caused by many common problems, such as heart disease or high blood pressure. It's very important that the patient be worked up for any diseases to make sure they're controlled. Men also need to make sure they're healthy enough to have sex. If they're not, Viagra won't give them a heart attack or kill them, but the exertion might.

Can it wreak havoc on your sex life? These drugs just enhance your normal physiology—they don't cause you to have a longer erection. The drugs only work if there is sexual stimulation. If a man's not in a stimulating situation, he's not going to get an erection.

The seven-hour erection is a myth—however, a side effect of Viagra can be priapism, which is an erection for more than four hours. It's a medical emergency that needs to be treated in the ER.

What are the benefits and drawbacks of using these types of drugs from an emotional perspective? The benefit is that they can enhance relationships—these drugs are helping the patient and the partner. There are two people involved when this drug is taken.

The drawback is that women may not necessarily want to have the increase in sexual activity—or the men may be seeking other partners (which is not as common with older partners).

Timing It Right

One of the most common questions I get from readers is, "How long should I wait before having sex with someone new?" (Actually, truth be told, this question comes primarily from women. With few exceptions, for most men the answer to the question, "How soon should you have sex?" is, "How soon can I get it?")

Obviously, the "right time" between two consenting adults varies with every relationship. Some people think it's okay to sleep with someone on the first date; others think nothing before marriage is acceptable. My own theory on the right time to do it for the first time falls somewhere in between tramp-o-rama and virgin nun.

If you're just looking for a wild night, and a serious relationship or pesky moral dilemmas aren't in the picture, then by all means, let the shirt buttons go flying. But if what you're looking for is a long-term relationship, you should wait to have sex until you're in an exclusive relationship, and then hold off on doing the deed for at least a month.

No Sex for the First Month. Really.

That's right. We put it in bold so you'd notice. Remember the old saying your mother or grandmother used to repeat? "Why buy the cow when you can get the milk for free?" Well, like it or not, in theory, it still holds true today. Sure, the sexual revolution has loosened things up a bit, but as we all know, that old double standard still exists. That's because our brains move a whole lot faster than our biology. Whip out the fur-lined handcuffs and edible undies on your honeymoon, if you're so inclined. The third date is not the time.

Okay, now try not to have a heart attack; it's really not that bad. Once you start dating someone exclusively, one more month really isn't that long to wait.

Why wait a month? The answer may surprise you. It has nothing to do with any moral issues, and it's not about playing hard to get. It's about chemistry. Brain chemistry.

The Love Drug

I mentioned oxytocin a bit earlier, but now I'd like to explain how it works. When women have sex, a chemical called oxytocin is released in our brains. Scientists refer to it as the "cuddle hormone." Why? Because it causes the affected person to get all sorts of mushy, googly, nesting, romantic feelings. Oxytocin is released in our bodies when we nurse to help us bond with our babies. It's also released when we have sex. Men get a rush of oxytocin as well, but in a much, much smaller amount. Conveniently for them, oxytocin is counteracted by testosterone. There is no such antidote for women.

This is one of the reasons men feel closer to women during sex (but not after). Once they get that burst of testosterone, they're ready to take a nice nap or go back to business as usual.

So what happens if you have sex too soon? A guy you thought was just so-so yesterday suddenly becomes Mr. Fabulous once you've had sex with him. Did he stop ending jokes with "get it," picking his nose, or talking incessantly about his mother/pet iguana/job at the post office? No. The difference is sex. Doped up on oxytocin, it's much more difficult, through the haze of googly-moogly romantic emotion, to judge whether or not he's someone you really want to be with.

The one-month sex embargo is just an extra measure of certainty to make sure the guy is really someone you want to be involved with on that level of intimacy. How long you wait is up to you, as long as you wait at least a month. After the one-month mark, it will be abundantly clear to your man that you do not take this sex thing lightly and that someone would have to be pretty darn special before you'd consider jumping into bed with him. And you will have the opportunity to make your decision while your brain is still functioning properly.

Don't worry if you think your guy will leave if you don't have sex with him. After interviewing hundreds of men on the subject, I can tell you that this simply isn't a factor. If he can't wait until you're ready, he certainly won't be hanging around long after the deed is done. By waiting, you are sending a message to your guy that sex with you is something special, and he will have no choice but to believe you are worth the wait.

Talking Dirty: How Soon Is Too Soon to Bring Up Sex Online?

I have a female friend who is frequently the target of men in search of the **quick-e**.

> **quick-e** (kwi-kE) *noun:* A situation in online dating in which one party makes sexual comments or suggestions within the first few emails. Or minutes. (In other words, way too soon.)

After a couple of "hi-how-are-yous," suddenly you find yourself on the receiving end of a nudie-cam transmission, or for the slightly more subtle letch, an inquiry as to your breakfast order.

You're looking for true love. They're looking for action.

For most men, it seems the topic of women bringing up sex too soon appears to be a nonissue. After months of inquiries, I was unable to locate even a single guy who found it a problem. But for women, the issue is big. Troublesome. Creepy.

E-ping Toms. Sex Scavengers. Internet Degenerates. From unseemly photos to body-part inquiries to the wolf in Prince Charming's clothing, female online daters are bombarded with inappropriate IMs, photos, and emails. An online dater from Baltimore sums it up: "I disregard those emails and write those prospects off. Imagine what a first date would be like if they were already lecherous just on email!"

To most women, sex talk too early on is the online-dating equivalent of Internet pharmacy spam clogging up your inbox. It's annoying and unwelcome, and we can't imagine that anyone would actually respond. Many women feel that guys who bring up bedroom talk right away are just looking for sex, or, worse yet, that they have terrible manners.

Most experts agree that when someone brings up sex right away, it should raise some red flags. Psychotherapist Wendy Allen says, "A man wanting sex too early has nothing to do with you. It's just his own persistent horniness. This transparency has given you a window into this person's motives."

For most women, immediate and unwelcome sex talk is repulsive. This sort of inappropriate contact is a sign of a poor social skills, disrespect, lack of impulse control, or boundary issues, and it is the quickest, easiest way to tell that a man is only looking for sex.

But how early is too early? If you've made it clear in your online profile that you're looking for a relationship or casual dating, anytime before the first few in-person meetings is too soon.

Mary Jo Fay, author of *Please Dear, Not Tonight: The Truth About Women and Sex,* warns, "If a guy mentions in a profile (in addition to his height, weight, job, loves, passions, etc.) that he enjoys lazy afternoons under the covers with someone he loves, that's one thing. But if he's sending a potential mate Web links to porn sites or sex toys, or is asking her what position she prefers, or invites her to have phone sex with him before even asking her about her likes, family, job, or expectations in a relationship, then he's really only looking for one thing. Period."

Not sure how to handle the dirty-talk issue? Well, if you wouldn't say something to someone you met at a wedding for the first time, you shouldn't say it to an online prospect. And if you find yourself a recipient of unwanted smut, the best plan is to (a) change the subject; (b) let the person know he's crossed a line; or (c) end the dialogue right away, and block his email.

Don't allow men using the implied anonymity of the Internet to disregard social filters that would normally be in place. The world (and online dating) work a lot better when we're all on our best behavior. And if you're the target of an Internet Degenerate, trust your instincts, and apply the same rules that you would in person. If a man you just met at a restaurant asked you to show him your bra three minutes after making your acquaintance, you'd throw a drink at him and ask the maitre d' to escort him to his car. The same rules apply online. Don't do it, and don't take it.

How to Tell If He's Just in It for Sex

He'll tell you.

Will he come right out and say, "Hey, I'm just in this for sex, and once you want something more, I'll be peeling my tires out of your driveway"? No, not usually. But he will tell you, and it will sound something like this:

- "I don't want to date anyone seriously right now." (This comes in many incarnations, but basically it's one of the common variations of, "I'm still getting over someone.")

- "I'm really busy at work."

- "You deserve someone who will want a relationship"

- 'I don't ever see myself getting married again."

- 'I don't want to hurt you."

- "I don't think I can be what you need."

Do not mistake the fact that he says one of the above to you and then has sex with you for a change of heart on his part. For him, sex seals the deal. It means you understand that he does not want a commitment, and you are complicit in the plan.

Don't assume his emotional stance has changed. Be sure to talk it over with him if some sort of emotional commitment is important to you. And do it before you "do it."

Letters to Lisa   ♥♥♥♥♥♥♥♥

Dear Lisa,

I met this guy online and we started talking on the phone and via email. Then, about a month into things, he started calling me and sending me IMs every day. I told him that I wanted a lover; he came over, and we slept together. Then I started acting needy, pestering him about what I mean to him, acting insecure, repeating myself, etc. One night, I even kept him on the phone for four hours out of insecurity. During that phone call, I asked him if he considered us to be dating. He didn't want to answer. I kept bugging him, and then he groaned and finally told me, "I just want to be your friend. You're not the kind of person I see myself in a committed relationship with. I'm sorry, and I don't want to hurt you." I was devastated. I think I'm in love with him.

I've already slept with him again. He came over about a week after "the phone call" (we had already made plans), and he was loving and friendly. That night we had sex, and it was as good as the first time, or even better. He didn't say anything about our phone conversation.

I can tell that he cares about me on some level. My question is, can I win him back? I want him. Is it possible at this point?

Lovesick Puppy

Dear Lovesick,

He didn't bring up your telephone conversation because for him, the issue has been resolved. He told you he doesn't see a future with you, and the fact that you had sex with him again tells him that's A-okay with you. He is now under the impression that you two are sex buddies, with no strings attached.

I'm a little bit confused about why you would tell this guy that you want a lover and then pull a Fatal Attraction *on him. If you want to be romantically involved with someone, don't sleep with him on the first date. And if you tell a guy you want sex before you've ever met in person, don't pull the old switcheroo on him the moment his pants are on the floor and ask him where the relationship is going.*

A four-hour neurosis fest with someone you barely know is a strong signal to me that you're not in an emotional state where you can be in a healthy relationship right now. I think you should talk to a counselor (and steer clear of dating) until you've worked out some of your insecurity issues. Otherwise, you'll either end up attracting guys who treat you like linoleum, or worse, send sweet, normal guys running for their lives.

Chalk this one up to experience, doll.

Best,

Lisa

If You're Just Looking for Sex

Sometimes you just want sex. Without all the mess that goes with it.

It is important to make sure your partner knows where you stand emotionally, but even if you are completely honest (as you should be), you may end up with some complications later.

Remember, we women tend to bond with men once we've slept with them, so be forthright about how you're feeling, and be prepared in case you have an emotional shift the morning after.

Sex Is Good for You

If the orgasms and naked men aren't enough of a draw, below you'll find nine more benefits of having regular sex.

1) **Sex makes you more fit.** Enthusiastic sex can burn up to two hundred calories, about the same as spending twenty minutes rollerblading or jogging on a treadmill. British researchers found that having sex three times a week for a year burns off the equivalent of six Big Macs. (Or four big slices from the Cheesecake Factory.)

2) **Sex is nature's Prozac.** A recent study from SUNY–Albany found that semen acts as an antidepressant: Women having sex without condoms had fewer signs of depression than women who didn't. (Have sex. Or skip condoms.) Word to the wise—the antidepressant benefits don't outweigh the STD risk, so be sure to practice safe sex unless you're in a committed, monogamous relationship.

3) **It makes you look better.** A study at Scotland's Royal Edinburgh Hospital found that women who were having sex four times a week looked an average of seven to twelve years younger than their not-so-active counterparts.

4) **It gives you better hair days.** Sex releases estrogen, which makes your hair shiny and your skin supple.

5) **It gives you better bladder control.** Sexual activity improves your Kegel muscles, which, in turn, give you

better bladder control. A boon for anyone who's ever experienced an unfortunate sneeze.

6) **It can cool down hot flashes.** Estrogen released during sex can help to alleviate (albeit temporarily) symptoms associated with perimenopause and menopause.

7) **It can cure migraines.** The magic combination of endorphins and corticosteroids during arousal and orgasm creates a painkiller that rivals even the really good prescription stuff.

8) **It fights colds and flu.** A recent study at Wilkes University says having sex once a week significantly boosts the immune system with higher levels of a health-preserving antibody called Immunoglobulin A.

9) **It gives you a better booty.** Having sex works your butt, thighs, pelvis, and arms. Especially your butt.

 Grown-Up Dating Fact

People whose health is excellent or very good are nearly twice as likely to be sexually active as those in poor or fair health.

Source: New England Journal of Medicine

Letters to Lisa

Dear Lisa,

I was seeing this guy for about three months. Things were going fairly well, but we didn't have a lot of time for each other. I told him that I wanted more of his time and that I felt he was just around for sex. He, of course, said it wasn't just about sex, but that we were both just really busy.

So we stopped seeing each other for a couple of weeks. Then I wanted to see him again, so I told him I would be more understanding about how busy he is, and I would try to make more time for him in my schedule. He said okay, but still we didn't see each other very often—and whenever we did, we had sex. Finally I told him I needed to know what was going on and what he really wanted—and if he didn't know, I couldn't wait around. He told me not to wait then. I asked him if he had been seeing anyone else, or if he was interested in seeing someone else, and he said no.

So I asked him why he feels like he can't be committed, because it seems like he has been for the last three months. Even though we decided to stop seeing each other, I feel like he is still interested but for some reason is holding back. I haven't been with or dated this guy in about two months, but I can't get him out of my mind. I really like him. What can I do to get him interested again?

Thanks,

Three–Month Stand

Dear Three-Month Stand,

Wow, this is a tough one. I don't think you're going to like what I have to say, but I'm going to give it to you straight. Sometimes when someone tells us something we don't really want to hear, we kind of gloss it over in our minds and hear only what we want to hear.

Clearly you have strong feelings for this guy, but I think you might not be hearing what he's telling you.

He has not been committed to you. He is squeezing you into his busy schedule for sex. If he had strong feelings for you, he would make time for you in his life in between the board meetings and reality TV. He is holding back, because he doesn't want a relationship with you (other than the one he currently has—a sexual relationship with no commitment). It's probably true that he's not interested in anyone else romantically, but he's not interested in you that way either. I think he's been trying to tell you that in every way he knows how.

That said, why in the world are you so devoted to a guy who is clearly not devoted to you? With very little encouragement, you have volunteered to be his girlfriend-on-call and rearrange your schedule so he can continue his lack of commitment to you. Why would you want to be with someone who clearly has no interest in being with you? You deserve better than that! There's a big difference between compromising for love and in BEING compromised. I'm afraid you're being compromised.

Make a pact with yourself to stop today. You're not a doormat; you're an amazing, unique woman, and you deserve to be loved and treated with respect.

Realize that you are worth more—much more—and don't settle for any man who doesn't treat you as such. A man who is in love with you will make time to be with you and will treat you well. In the future, I'd let your dates pursue you a little. That way, you'll know what their interests are before you commit your heart.

Best,

Lisa

Chapter 10

Born-Again Virgins

After a divorce, the death of your spouse, or a long period of celibacy, the idea of sleeping with someone new can be a really scary proposition. Sometimes we feel like it's been so long, we might have forgotten how it's done. What's important to remember is that sex doesn't have to be perfect to be good. Sometimes it doesn't even have to be that good to be good.

When you're considering sleeping with someone new, treat yourself gently and go at your own pace.

3 Things to Carry in Your Purse If You Think You Might Be Up for a Big Night In

1. Condoms (you don't want to have him running to the drugstore in the middle of the action)

2. Baby wipes (they can be carried in a small plastic bag in your purse, and you can use them to freshen up anywhere that needs it—including armpits or those morning-after mascara-raccoon eyes)

3. A toothbrush

Don't allow yourself to feel pressured to have sex after a certain amount of time or number of dates. Try not to overthink it. If it's been a long time, you're bound to have some emotion around the experience, and that's okay. Do what you can to relax and enjoy yourself (a glass of wine can help), and let nature take its course from there.

Dimmer Switches and Other Genius Inventions: Sex Tips for Born-Again Virgins

Whether it's the first time you're having sex in eleven years or just the first time with him, below you'll find some pointers on how to lose your inhibitions without losing your cool.

Don't Spend the Night

If it's been a while, you're bound to have a lot of emotions afterwards. Give yourself a chance to deal.

Use a Condom

There are lots of new diseases since your last time around. Protect yourself. And yes, I know I sound like a broken record.

Don't Worry About Your Droopy Butt

You may be older, but your partner probably is, too. Nobody expects you to be perfect. That's what the dimmer switch is for.

Does It Always Make That Sound?

Sex is sometimes messy, sometimes loud, and sometimes embarrassing. Get over yourself if you haven't already. It's part of the package.

Will Everything Work the Way It's Supposed To?

Probably. If not, enjoy yourself anyway. You may discover something new.

Other Genius Inventions

If you're on antidepressants or thyroid medication, or if your estrogen level has begun to taper off, you may find that you're not as sensitive or that you have trouble reaching orgasm. Arousal creams, called "heighteners," help stimulate blood flow and increase arousal, sensitivity, and overall sensation for women without nine hours of foreplay. (Try Ex-T-Cee from Pure Romance, www.pureromance.com.)

> **"We all want to recapture the excitement of our frisky twenties, but when we get older, it can sometimes be a little bit harder to turn that arousal switch on and off at just the drop of a hat. We have so many responsibilities and stress factors, which can disrupt intimacy and often get in the way of achieving desire. This is not to say that sex isn't good in your forties; in fact, sex can often be better! One way to speed things up is through an arousal cream: Its mood-altering qualities will give you a sensual boost and kick-start the arousal process."**
> **—Patty Brisben,**
> **founder of Pure Romance**

Letters to Lisa ♥♥♥♥♥♥♥

Dear Lisa,

I met a man online, and we had a great emotional and intellectual connection. We talked for hours on the computer, shared pictures, and developed a physical attraction, and then we began talking by phone.

It was very fast and intense. We jumped into a committed relationship, shared very personal and intimate information, made very committed statements and plans—and then suddenly, he stopped.

For a week, I couldn't get a hold of him. I would call: no answer. I would leave messages: no return phone calls. So I tried his email: still no answers to my questions.

I wondered if something bad had happened—maybe an emergency—but still no response.

So I gave up. I wrote a nice email that stated I wasn't sure what was going on and wondered if he could just give me an explanation. I also said he was a great guy and wished him well in all aspects of his life.

I told him I figured he wanted out, and instead of just telling me, he was taking the cowardly way out—and I didn't want to deal with it.

Then, he responded back. He said he was sorry for the way he acted, and he had no excuse. He was scared and confused, because he didn't think it was healthy to have such strong feelings for me and think about me all the time when we hadn't even met yet. He said he was losing control over his emotions, and he's always in control of his emotions. He hoped I could find it in my heart to forgive him and be friends.

I guess my question is now, what does he want? He hasn't contacted me since the email. Some of my male friends say that my email was quite a blow, and maybe he feels he can't contact me again.

I miss him. I especially miss the great connection we had, and I do feel a little ashamed at my response, because while I feel my feelings were valid, I don't believe in attacking people and their character. I just feel he still didn't give me a clear-cut answer. Maybe I don't want to see it.

Sincerely,

Heart Online

Dear Online,

I think it's pretty clear what he wants. And you're right—you don't want to see it. He wants a hot and heavy email/phone gig but doesn't want to show up in person. I'm guessing he's a married guy who thinks it's not cheating if he doesn't see the color of your panties. (Even if you already described them on a phone date.)

Cut him loose. You're associating your initial chemistry with actual attachment. Don't focus so much on the initial sparks, but instead consider his appallingly immature behavior.

If you're looking for love over the long haul, do you honestly think the guy who can't keep an Internet date is going to be reliable enough to take out the trash, much less be stable enough to maintain a real relationship? I'm thinking no.

Best,

Lisa

Seven Tips for Choosing a Good Lubricant

As we age, hormone changes cause us to lose some of our natural lubrication. To keep sex fun and pain-free, Michael Alvear, host of HBO's *Sex Inspectors* and creator of Blabbermash.com—the YouTube of sex and dating advice—offers these tips on what to look for when choosing a personal lubricant.

- **Texture and smoothness:** You don't want it to be sticky or tacky (a snotlike texture is bad).

- **How long it lasts:** Like most of the men you date, you want your lubrication to stick around for more than a minute and a half.

- **The kind of container it comes in:** You want it to be so easy to open, you can open it with your feet. If it takes two hands, you have interrupted the action. Alvear says, "Stay away from jars and tubs—they tend to collect pubic hair." (Say it with me, "*Ewww.*")

- **The wash-off factor:** Oil-based lubes like Vaseline, Crisco (really, Crisco?), and baby oil are tough to get off—you need lots of soap and water. You don't want that "You're soaking in it, Madge" feeling. Silicone-based lubricants have a lot of great properties, but are more expensive—and you have to use soap to wash them off. Most water-based lubes can wash off with water.

- **Taste and smell:** Be sure to check this out, even if the lubricant is unscented. Some smell bad—like a hospital or a butcher shop. Scent should definitely enter into the equation.

- **The irritation factor:** The two ingredients that are most likely to cause irritation are nonoxynol-9 (a spermicide, which, according to the World Health Organization, may actually increase your risk for contracting HIV) and glycerine (a form of sugar found in a lot of lubricants that taste sweet). If you have sensitive or delicate skin, or you're getting rashes, itches, or odd bumps, lubricants containing either of these two ingredients may be the culprit.

- **Temperature:** Some lubricants create heat; some create coolness. As many of us know, the ones that create heat can be magic for the ladies. Heat is a really important thing to put us in the mood—it stimulates blood flow, which is a precursor to stimulation. That's why sitting in a warm bath can sometimes put you in the mood for romance.

On picking a lubricant, Alvear advises, "Three words: test, test, test." Alvear also suggests that there's no need to spend a fortune testing lubricants—many online stores, such as Condomania.com, offer sample packs, and bedroom home-party companies such as Pure Romance (www.pureromance.com) will allow you to smell, taste, and skin-test a variety of lubricants and other goodies.

Size-Twelve Sex

There are a lot of women having sex with the lights off. (Or with the dimmer switch turned all the way down.)

We're afraid our stomachs pooch or jiggle too much; our butts are too big; or our breasts are too saggy or not the right size (or not the *same* size).

Most of us women are insecure about our bodies, whether we're overweight, underweight, or damned near perfect. We obsess about our shortcomings in excruciating detail. (Which always cracks me up, because a hairy, overweight guy with a four-inch member that leans to the left would happily have sex with a gorgeous woman in the middle of a stadium filled with people without a second thought, if the opportunity presented itself.)

We worry that a man who has sprung for nine dinners, put the charm on full blast, and worked so hard for the last seventeen days to get our clothes *off* will invariably be disappointed once we ditch the push-up bra and super-duper spandex tummy tourniquet and wish we'd put them back *on*.

So we leave the lights off. Hide under the covers. Avoid certain positions, because of the "jiggle factor." Instead of trusting he'll find desire in the midst of our cellulite, our extra flesh, our imperfections, we hope the darkness will camouflage our flaws and leave him with the slimmer visual image we attempt to project when we encase our insecurities in Lycra and industrial-strength undergarments.

And for every woman who is having "nookie noir," there are lots of others who are subsisting on carrot curls, Lean Cuisines, and never-ending bouts with an elliptical machine, feeling like they won't be eligible for the grand prize of happiness, true love, or the really good deals on designer handbags until they hit their target weight.

Who among us hasn't felt certain at one time or another that our lives would surely improve significantly, if only we could lose that twenty pounds and slip into a pair of size-six jeans?

One female dater says, "I'm a size-twelve woman in the dating pool. I do think the majority of men are looking for smaller 'perfect' women to date. The challenge is, quite frankly, that there are even fewer men who could meet the same standards; so why should women starve themselves, work out religiously, and get plastic surgery, when men won't go to the same lengths? Once a man does give a woman who is size twelve or larger a chance, the man is usually happy with the way she looks. It is getting past that initial first impression and expectation that is very difficult."

Plus-size models usually wear a size twelve. The average Canadian and American woman wears a size fourteen. Does it strike anyone else as strange that our "plus-size" models are smaller than our real people?

Jennifer Weiner, the best-selling author of *Good in Bed*, says, "There are very few representations in the media of 'every-woman.' We are living in the age of the incredible shrinking starlet (Mary-Kate and Ashley Olsen, Paris Hilton, Nicole Richie). With all these bony little actresses, if you're a size twelve (or bigger), you have no one representing you in the media. Ugly Betty is *maybe* a size ten.

"There's not a lot of diversity—it worries me as a woman, as a mother—not having larger women [in the media] that are leading lives that include things *other* than dieting and despair."

It is important for our self-esteem to have icons and role models who look like us. If we don't, we begin to believe the way we look is wrong. I often wonder if the next generation will grow up without any clue about what real breasts look like. If anemic, rich, blonde, and busty is the standard we hold ourselves to, how can any of us feel good about how we look?

Has fake become the new real?

Yes. But real women are more appealing than we give ourselves credit for.

Weiner's novels feature heroines who are real, genuine, wise-cracking, intelligent, likeable, desirable, capable, and, in her words, "big girls." They are the women I'd choose as my friends.

And whether you believe it or not, they are the women men choose as their girlfriends.

But we tend to be hardest on ourselves.

One male dater, Anthony, says, "I really think that women are concerned about their bodies *way* more than men. Guys know that the perfect body does not exist, and the pictures in the magazines have been altered, from hair color, neckline, skin tone to weight. I have never met a woman who was less attractive once the clothes came off."

According to another, Harry, "If there is a little fat, so what? It's what's on the inside that counts. As for my girlfriend—yes, she is very concerned about her weight. I think it involves more her ego than anything else. Although, I try to reassure her that I think she is beautiful. Size does not matter to me. Having a good head on your shoulders, a good heart, and a great pair of lips is what I look for in a woman."

Philip says, "What it all hinges on, regardless of weight (attraction isn't on a sliding scale), is whether I'm inspired by her. Surprised by her charm. She could be my muse. To love this way, and be loved the same way in return, is something everyone should experience. Once you get this far, what they look like, clothes off, seems entirely trivial."

Here's a news flash, ladies: Guys aren't settling for fat-dumpy-imperfect ol' you because they can't score the stick-thin supermodels. They. Don't. Care.

One dater, Katherine, says, "As a size-twelve woman who is five-foot-nine, I am in no way challenged in dating or slighted by my body. I look normal, slightly athletic, [and] would allow that I'm fairly attractive. I'm in no way a stick-thin model, but neither am I grotesquely obese or even largely overweight. I've had many boyfriends ask me why I stress so much about trying to fit into even smaller jeans, because to them it doesn't make any sense."

Weiner says, "A lot of it is attitude. Men think, *We don't care if you're not perfect—we just want to see you naked either way.* Men have their own insecurities: about their looks, how much money they're making. If you're feeling good about where you are—if you're happy, confident—you'll have a better shot at meeting someone. And that's true for big girls and skinny girls."

So ladies, keep those lights on. Let your thighs jiggle and your boobs swing free. It's time to start focusing on your own enjoyment, on being in the moment, on enjoying sex for all it is. Stop worrying about your cellulite and just have fun.

Otherwise, what's the point?

Chapter 11

Condoms and Other Mood Killers

Condoms are just as awkward as you remember, but they are a fact of modern dating and more crucial than ever.

I realize that I have mentioned this fact in about five previous chapters, but your health and well-being are important to me. So I'm just going to gently remind you one last time. (Okay, maybe two last times.)

Modern STDs can kill you at worst and leave you itchy and foul at best. Most all of them can be prevented by using a condom.

Condoms come in lovely colors that glow in the dark or match your wallpaper. They are scented or flavored or sparkly and are available in a variety of sizes. They are your best defense to keep yourself healthy.

Please use one.

Men, as you probably already know, will occasionally resist using condoms.

Tell your partner that no condom means no sex. Period.

He will use one, even if he whines about it. Because sex with a condom is way better than no sex at all.

If you prefer to have unprotected sex (who doesn't?), get tested, and make sure you're in a committed and absolutely monogamous relationship. Otherwise, make condoms the rule.

Remember, condoms aren't nearly the mood-killers that STDs are.

Always, always, always use a condom until you are both (1) in a long-term, monogamous relationship, and (2) tested and found to be free of STDs.

If it freaks you out to buy condoms at the local Kroger with your yogurt and salad-by-the-pound, by all means order yourself a box from one of the many online drugstores. They'll deliver right to your door, and even your postal worker won't suspect a thing.

Letters to Lisa ❤❤❤❤❤❤❤❤

Dear Lisa,

I have been trying hard to follow what I think should be the rules for dating, even though I made the initial contact through an online service. He asked for my picture after I contacted him, hinting that he wasn't interested in a long-distance relationship. Once he saw my picture, though, he was very interested; he said he conducts business in my town and asked me out. We have been dating for two months but only see each other once or twice a week, because we live ninety miles apart.

I always go to his place (a large city), because I am dating someone else in my small town—who I would have a good possibility of running into—and because I don't want to bring a parade of men into my house with my son present.

Here's the second issue: I have had sex with him, but not on the first date. We do tons of things together; I never call him; he always calls and emails me first, pays for everything, opens doors, etc. However, the sex thing is bothering me. I think that it was too soon, and he might think I am easy.

Also, on our first date, we were discussing relationships, and he said that any relationship he would be in now would be a "transitional one," because he had only been divorced a year. However, he did ask me recently how I thought "we" were doing. I gave a rather noncommittal answer, and he said that it would be very easy for him to be in love with me. (Unspoken was that he isn't in love NOW.) Is there a way that I can backtrack but still let him know I'm interested? I also am uncomfortable with the sex and want to know how I can get out of that without him thinking I am losing interest.

Sincerely,

Wondering

Dear Wondering,

First off, let me just say that at any time, in any relationship, you can (and should) stop having sex whenever you want to. If you're not comfortable, then don't do it. Bottom line. Don't worry so much about whether or not he'll think you're losing interest. If all other signs suggest otherwise and he's a nice guy, he'll hang in there until you're ready. As for whether or not he thinks you're easy because you slept with him a little earlier than you'd planned—well, all I can say is, he'll know differently when you start your sex sabbatical. If he really likes you, he'll stay. If he's just in it for sex, he'll probably hit the road, but frankly, he'd be doing you a favor—you wouldn't want that kind of guy around anyway.

As for always going to his place, I do think that sets up an unfair standard, but I can see why you wouldn't want him to come to your place. A good compromise might be to meet him at a place that's halfway between your cities (preferably a bit closer to your side of the border).

I'm assuming that the other person you're dating in your town is a more casual relationship. Obviously, you'll want to be cautious about dating more than one person, especially if you're sleeping with one of them.

Don't worry so much about letting him know you're interested. You have been dating him for a while, after all, and frankly a little bit of uncertainty can make a man set his priorities straight. If you stop doing all the work to keep the relationship afloat, he'll do one of two things: If he wants to be with you, he'll start picking up the slack; if he's indifferent and just dating you because it's convenient, he'll let you slip away. Either way, you'll be in a much better position than you are now.

Kisses,

Lisa

Chapter 12

The Secret Bedroom Technique That Makes Men Propose Right Away

Give Yourself a Second Chance to Be a Blushing Bride

It may not be a popular thing to say, but it is the truth: Men are primarily motivated by sex.

I don't want to bore you with the details, but this is rooted in evolutionary psychology (and if you're as fascinated by this topic as I am, you might want to read *Why Beautiful People Have More Daughters*). Basically, it works like this: Every action men take—the reason to gain more power, more money, more status—all of it is rooted in their desire to have more access to more women to have—you guessed it—more sex.

Now before you start snorting and thinking what basic animals men are, you should know, they are biologically programmed to do this, just as you are biologically programmed to make your home pretty and comfortable and bond with your girlfriends. These things have a purpose for us as human beings, and generally speaking, Mother Nature knows what she's doing.

Can we rise above our biology? Absolutely. Is it easier to just work along with it? Definitely.

That said, if you're looking to get married again, I'd like to let you in on a little secret.

Holding off on sex speeds up the courtship process.

Sure, it seems counterintuitive. But a man will propose much more quickly if he knows that the sex won't happen until after the wedding or engagement. I've seen it happen time and time again. And the benefit to you, of course, is that you get to evaluate the relationship on the emotional connection, before your brain is swimming in oxytocin and orgasms.

The downside, of course, is that if the sex is lackluster, you're sort of stuck with the guy.

Just thought you'd like to know.

Part 3

Get Married

Chapter 13

Shacking Up: 3 Out of 4 Ministers Say You Probably Won't Go to Hell

Should you live together? Or get married?

Many women over forty are opting out of marriage. Maybe you've been married before, and you're not interested in risking your finances on such a sketchy investment. Maybe you're sure about wanting a commitment, but not positive about taking it all the way to the justice of the peace. Maybe he lives in Tuscaloosa, Alabama, and you don't want to uproot yourself and leave your fabulous life in Seattle.

Whether you're not sure what you want and you're just looking for more of a test drive or you've weighed your options and decided marriage is not for you, living together might be the solution you're looking for. On the positive side, living together can offer you the commitment and shared responsibilities you're looking for. On the flip side, if you're settling for cohabitation when what you really want is marriage, your best option might be to stay where you are. Why? Studies show that couples who live together are less likely to get married. And for couples who do live together without the intention of getting married (as in, merely for convenience or financial issues), their odds of getting a divorce are higher if they eventually do marry.

Things to Consider Before You Remarry

We've all heard that the odds for success in a second or third marriage go down dramatically, but what you may not know is that there are a number of other factors that can hurt or improve your chances for success.

- **Get your degree.** A college education improves your odds for staying married.

- **Try not to get married more than twice.** A second marriage increases your odds for divorce, but not by much (3 percent for middle-class couples). But the odds of divorce go up dramatically with each subsequent marriage.

- **Keep your own place.** Those couples who live together with the intention of getting married have a lower divorce rate than those who just move in together without a plan.

- **Sign up for a marriage class.** Couples who attend premarital classes or counseling slash their odds of divorce by almost a third.

- **Find a guy slightly richer than you are.** Women who earn more than their husbands have an increased risk of divorce. (Although this may be because they have the resources to leave if things get bad, and not necessarily because making more money causes problems within the marriage.)

- **Well, there's really nothing you can do about this one.** You're more likely to get divorced if your parents are divorced.

- **Try to get along with your dad. Or alternatively, your spouse's dad.** If you have a bad relationship with your father, you're more likely to get divorced. (According to an article in *Time* magazine, this risk can be counteracted if you have a good relationship with your groom's family. It's one heck of an incentive to be nice to your new mother-in-law.)

- **Don't cheat.** Richer couples divorce over personality conflicts, such as incompatibility or communication issues, while poorer couples divorce over physical abuse, substance addiction, and money problems. Infidelity is a deal breaker for everybody, rich and poor.

- **Go to church as much as your spouse does.** Being religious doesn't statistically make you any happier in your marriage, but it can lower your likelihood of divorce if religion is equally important to both of you.

- **Money makes a difference.** Remember the old saying about falling in love with a poor man and marrying a rich one? Turns out, it's not too far off base. A household income of $50,000 or more gives you and your spouse a 68 percent chance of remaining married for at least fifteen years.

Source: Rutgers Marriage Project and Time Magazine

Should You Relocate for Love?

Whether you met online or at an out-of-town sales conference, a lot of couples are finding themselves madly in love with someone who lives seven states away. If you're considering relocating to take the relationship to the next level, keep these things in mind before you rent the U-Haul.

- **A Fresh Start:** There's something exciting about leaving your old life behind and embarking on a new life and a new relationship.

- **Move or Die:** Generally speaking, long-distance relationships have to come to a sort of fruition, or they'll die out. You can't go on forever with no plans to be in the same location in the future. It just doesn't work. Eventually, you'll have to decide if the relationship is a keeper or not.

- **Career Crushers:** How will the move affect your career, and is that a risk you're willing to take?

- **Money Matters:** Who pays the difference when one partner moves to a city that is much more expensive? Who pays for relocation expenses?

- **Losing Your Support Base:** Once you make the move, you may feel isolated. If you and your partner have a disagreement, all of your girlfriends will be five hundred miles away, which makes commiserating over margaritas a bit of a challenge. Plus, it can take weeks or months of your life to find a new gyno, dentist, vet, and hairstylist.

- **Liking His Friends.** If you're moving to where he is, his friends are about to become your friends. If you love them, great. But if you can't stand them, brace yourself, they're about to become a far bigger part of your life.

- **You Are My Everything:** When one partner relocates to a new city, it can put a lot of pressure on the relationship. While you are established, with friends and a routine, he might feel dependent on you to entertain him and provide most of his social structure, which can put a huge strain on the relationship. And vice versa if you move to where he is.

When deciding whether or not to live with someone, keep in mind what works best for you and your partner. Don't worry about what your relatives or the people at your church have to say about it—do what's right for you and your relationship.

Jan Dahlin Geiger, certified financial planner and author of *Get Your Assets in Gear! Smart Money Strategies,* answers tough questions for women considering marriage or remarriage.

After forty-five, is it smarter to get married or to live together?

It all depends on whether you want a contract or a commitment, in my opinion. If your attitude about marriage is that it is a contract, that you will only stay in it as long as everything is going your way, then for sure you are smarter to live together, never get married, and keep all your money separate. All you have to do is consider the cost of divorce, as well as the emotional wreckage, to know it makes more sense to stay single and not commingle money.

However, if your attitude is that marriage is a commitment and you are both committed to doing whatever it takes to make it work, it makes a lot more sense to get married and to combine finances. There is incredible synergy that I see with my clients who are happily married that you never, ever see with couples that are in more of a contract situation. You definitely see 1 + 1 = 5. I have seen newly married couples who decide it is important to get out of debt and start saving serious money, and it is incredible how much they can accomplish in just five years, working together.

Should you have a prenup?

It all depends on how much money is at stake and where you stand on the contract-versus-commitment issue. If there is a disparity in assets of $1 million or more and the couple is older than forty, a prenup can make sense. However, it is important to remember that the law of attraction is really powerful. Any prenup assumes you will probably get divorced, and you are planning for it. I tell my clients if they think they need a prenup, they probably should not marry that person.

Of course, if you are a billionaire like Paul McCartney, it makes sense to have a prenup for the simple reason that you will waste millions in legal fees otherwise.

There is a much, much easier solution that gives the same outcome for most people. That is, always keep any money you had prior to your marriage in separate accounts. Each person should have a net-worth statement prepared as of the day before the marriage. So say Sally has $300K in her 401(k), $200K in personal savings, and $100K in equity in her house. Harry has $200K in his 401(k), $100K in personal savings, and $100K equity in his house. They each do a net-worth statement to document this.

After the marriage, they each sell their homes. They use the $200K as a down payment on the new house, which they own jointly. Sally continues to keep $200K in her own name; Harry keeps $100K in his own name. They begin a new joint-savings account together with money they earn after the marriage. In the event of a divorce, all the money they had prior to the marriage is "off the table" in terms of negotiation, since they can document that they owned it prior to the marriage. More than likely, what they accumulate after the marriage will be split fifty-fifty in the event of a divorce.

Likewise, if Sally gets an inheritance during the marriage, she should keep it in her name only and document the amount received. Divorce laws clearly state that you keep your own inheritance, so long as it was never combined into a joint account.

What are the special considerations if you have children?

Again, a lot depends on how much money is at stake. If there is a lot of money, you need to be careful to set up your wills correctly. Most people will set it up so that if they die, what they own separately will go into a trust for the benefit of their children, with the income from the trust paid to the surviving spouse during his or her lifetime. Sometimes it makes sense to get a life-insurance policy, put it in an ILIT (irrevocable life insurance trust), and have that money go to the spouse so that the assets can go directly to the children. There are a million variations on what you can do—much depends on the couple's ages and the amount of money at stake.

I remarried at forty-three. My prior marriage was miserable. This one is going on sixteen years, and it is beyond fabulous. We were really clear that we wanted to make a commitment and do whatever was necessary to make it work, and we spent several years in counseling in the early years of our marriage.

Our net worth today is 1,000 percent of what it was fifteen and a half years ago when we married. We both bring out the best in each other. My husband today makes more than triple what he made when we married, and he credits me with a lot of that—nothing better than living with a full-time encourager and cheerleader.

So much of marriage is what you decide to make of it. Whatever you think about is going to grow. So if you don't trust the other person and think you need to be really careful about protecting your money, you will likely divorce eventually. If you treat the other person like he is magnificent, most people will grow into that expectation.

What are some of the smartest steps to take before getting married?

I definitely would document net worth prior to the marriage, and I would never combine premarriage assets. However, there is a certain amount of at least acting like you trust the other person needed to really grow a healthy, thriving, and wonderful marriage. The key thing is to be sure you are comfortable with the other person's character before you marry. If he tells you stories about cutting corners and trying to screw other people, it is just a matter of time until you are the screwee. If he tells you things and demonstrates things that show honesty and integrity, he is good marriage material!

The Grown-Up Bottom Line: It's always smart to speak with a financial advisor about your options before you book the caterer.

"I Don't Want To Die Alone" and 5 Other Horrible Reasons to Get Married

While there are lots of great reasons to get married, there are also some bad ones. Before you consider a trip down the aisle, make sure you're not heading in the wrong direction.

1. **You want someone else to support you financially.** Unwillingness to support yourself or fear of taking care of yourself is not a good reason to get married. Suck it up, girlfriend. It's time to start taking care of yourself.

2. **You are afraid to be alone.** Anyone who's been trapped in a bad relationship can tell you that being alone is a whole lot better than being with the wrong guy. Trust yourself, and be brave. You don't need a man.

3. **He really loves you, and he's a decent man. But you don't love him.** You can't learn to love someone. You might learn to tolerate him or even respect him, but you can't learn to love someone you don't love. The fact that he loves you a lot can't make up for the fact that you don't love him. Trust me.

4. **He needs a green card.** Aside from being illegal, this is really not a good reason to get married. But you already knew that.

5. **You think a legal commitment will improve your relationship.** Many women (and men) have believed this to be true. Unfortunately, a big party and a piece of paper will not make a bad relationship good. It won't even make a mediocre relationship good. Generally speaking,

time and marriage will only intensify the feelings that you have now: If your relationship makes you feel insecure, marriage will make you more insecure; if your guy drives you crazy with his incessant negativity, it will be ten times worse in ten years. A wedding can't fix a broken relationship. Not even the perfect wedding.

Letters to Lisa   ♥ ♥ ♥ ♥ ♥ ♥ ♥ ♥

Hi Lisa,

I've just ended a rocky two-year relationship with this guy who is wonderful. I fully believe he is "the one," but he has really bad habits and depression that I can't help him with. He got depressed, and he said that he was not ready to have a relationship but that he loves me so much. I believe him. It is really hard to go out with a person for two years and then not see him or talk to him at all. Any advice on how I should move on? And how can I approach him after I get over him to see if there is any possibility of reconciliation?

Thank you very much,

Sadly

Dear Sadly,

I'm so sorry about your breakup. I know it's difficult. Sometimes, however, it's not the person we miss so much as it is being part of a couple. And after a few months, that feeling either subsides, or we try to find a replacement partner. (Which may or may not be a good thing, depending on how much you've healed from the trauma of the breakup.)

Here's what I noticed upon reading your letter: It's full of contradictions. The relationship was rocky, but you believe he is "the one." He's a wonderful guy, but he has really bad habits. How do you get over him, but also, how can you approach him for reconciliation?

Sometimes I get too much information in a letter, and sometimes not nearly enough; this is one of those times when there's not enough. I just am not sure exactly what we're dealing with. When you say "really bad habits," do you mean he's dizzy on rum and Coke by 7:00 a.m. and sets your clothes on fire? Or that he leaves the toilet seat up or sometimes forgets to empty the litter box?

Let's deal with what we do know.

He's ended the relationship using a classic breakup line designed to spare your feelings. So from that, we know he wants out of the relationship.

You talk frequently about his depression (and its effect on your relationship) in your letter, so we know that (1) it's an ongoing problem, and it doesn't appear that he's managing it with medication or therapy; and (2) there's probably some pattern of bad behavior in the relationship you've excused because of the fact that he's suffering from depression.

You're right when you say that you can't help him with his depression. If you're concerned about his well-being, you might try suggesting he visit one of the many websites about depression and depression treatments. Or you can request information yourself and put it in his hands. However, you need to deal with the possibility that he will not act. Frankly, only he can deal with it, and quite honestly, you don't want to be in a relationship with him if he's not interested in finding a way to manage it. Why? There will be nothing you can do

202 *How to Date Like a Grown-Up*

to bring him up, but the depression, and more specifically, the results of actions caused by his depression, will most certainly drag both of you down together.

As for how you can deal with your heartbreak, you need to cut yourself loose from this relationship and consider it over. By all means, mourn for what has been lost, but move on with your life and goals. Don't bide your time, waiting for the day when you can reconcile. Consider this chapter closed, and move forward. If the two of you are truly meant to be together, two things will happen. First, he'll get help for his depression. And second, once he does, he'll approach you to put things back together. Unfortunately that could take years, and it's not healthy for you to put your life on hold waiting for "what ifs."

Let him go.

For more information on depression and treatment for depression, visit the National Foundation for Depressive Illness (www.depression.org)

Best of luck. I'm pulling for you.

Best,

Lisa

Chapter 14

Here Come the Grooms

Remember how so many of the women you knew in your twenties and thirties were clamoring to get married? Well, the tables have turned, and it is now men in their forties, fifties, and sixties who are scrambling for a trip down the aisle. And increasingly, women over forty are finding they like the single life just fine, thankyouverymuch.

Contrary to what many of my girlfriends believe, men do not marry for free laundry service. According to studies and my own interviews with marriage-minded men, guys want companionship and intimacy. They want the emotional, intellectual, and, of course, physical presence of a woman. This emotional desire to find a partner seems to increase as they get older—men don't want to be alone. They find themselves bored with the singles scene and looking to find someone to share their lives with.

Here's the rub. Many women over forty have already been married, have raised (or are raising) their children on their own, have built their lives and careers around a circle of friends, family, community and colleagues, and come to the conclusion that they like things just the way the are. Man-free.

Personally, I know a number of single women who have purchased homes together, and I have to say, it seems to work out pretty well for everyone. Aside from no longer throwing away their rent money, there are lots of other benefits as well:

They trade off cooking responsibilities, take turns doing the yard work, and with all women in the house, nobody is insisting on putting an ugly plaid recliner smack in the middle of the formal living room. Sounds like domestic bliss to me.

Why else are women deciding life is easier without a man in it? It depends on the individual, of course, but the thing I hear time and time again goes along the lines of, "I just don't want to deal with some guy's crap."

The good news is that, as they age, men deal with a lot of their own crap. Their testosterone decreases as they age, and they become a softer, cuddlier version of their former selves. They're still men, of course. The still leave their dirty underwear balled up on the bathroom sink, stack pizza boxes next to an over-flowing trash can instead of just taking it out, and occasionally have trouble sorting through their own emotions.

The most perceptible difference is that, as they mature, men become more enamored by the idea of marriage, while women, ironically, become less so.

Grown-Up Dating Fact

According to the Census Bureau, more than 75 percent of divorced and widowed baby boomers will marry again.

What Are Men Looking for in a Wife?

Raise your hand if you said "a nurse." In some respects, this is true. Many men over fifty are looking for someone to take care of them as they age. Raise your hand if you just blurted out "beauty." You may be surprised to know that a recent study of men (called VoiceMale) showed that, while beauty attracts, the most important factors men look for in a future wife are a positive outlook and self-confidence. Also high on the list were brains (hallelujah!), self-respect, motherliness, and for some, devotion to faith. Most of all, men are looking for companionship.

What Are You Looking for in a Husband?

Most grown-up women want to marry for companionship as well. The good news about marrying after forty is that some hardworking first wife may have already done the heavy lifting to help your future husband reach his full potential. Your groom-to-be probably already knows how to put the toilet seat down, that husbands are required to clean up the kitchen after a big holiday dinner, and that flowers, gifts, and a nice dinner out for anniversaries and birthdays are mandatory for marriage maintenance.

Men who marry later in life tend to be more open-minded, more willing to communicate, and more conscious of their wives' feelings.

Or sometimes they're just cranky old men.

Don't worry; you'll be able to tell the difference.

Seeking Mr. Clean

Studies at Ohio State University found that the more evenly household chores were distributed, the happier wives were with the marriage. Before you walk down the aisle, make sure your guy knows how the vacuum works. And if you're wondering how to motivate your groom to do more around the house, tell him there's nothing sexier in the world than watching a man unload the dishwasher.

To Marry or Not to Marry?

Be true to yourself. If marriage is something you're looking for, know that your pool of potential grooms is increasing by the day. And if you've come to the conclusion that you'd like to keep your life the way it is, with a side of male companionship and sex, you're sure to find a number of willing partners (even if they *would* rather take things to the next level).

The good news is that your day has come—the options are yours. You can create your romantic relationships to order, and build your life just the way you want it.

Letters to Lisa ♥♥♥♥♥♥♥♥

Hi Lisa,

I'm fifty-one and was married at, gulp, twenty the first time 'round. Divorced at thirty-five. Then married again at forty-two. (And, sadly, lost my beloved last year to cancer—widowed at fifty. UGH.) And for me, the second marriage was the real union—versus the weird playacting that occurred in my first marriage, which I refer to as the "Stepford Years."

When I married so young, I seemed to fall into the connect-the-dots mode of doing everything that was expected of me. The trouble in that marriage was that I held back my true self, and we weren't truly bonded with one another. A lack of maturity and self-awareness was mostly to blame, I reckon.

My second marriage, by stark contrast, came as a result of meeting the right man at the right time—after seven years on my own, fully rolling in a satisfying career and having a bevy of great friends (including close men friends). So it was all about creating a vibrant partnership that made every area of each of our lives better, and *richer*. He too had been in a fifteen-year marriage (both our spouses left us, by the way), and he had been on his own for three years. So we each knew we wanted that closeness again, and we were also very wired for commitment.

Because we were so fully formed as individuals and adults at that point in our lives (he was forty-nine), there was no game playing, nor was there any notion of anyone wanting or needing to "change" any key aspect about the other. My lofty ambition was to get him into a better-looking pair of eyeglasses, but once that was nailed, he was virtually perfect to me! We also developed a rather hilarious style of conflict resolution that made even some potentially tense moments times of laughter and bonding, as we navigated our way in this complicated world—including the stress of me trying to acclimate to stepmotherhood of his sullen fifteen-year-old son. This marriage was so successful because our backgrounds, tastes, lifestyle, and values were so closely aligned. And while our temperaments were quite different, we blended so well (about 95 percent of the time, a darned fine thing when you can actually pull it off). Our life together was defined by having a strong sense of being a team, sharing goals ("schemes 'n' dreams"), and enjoying the daylights out of each other.

My lost hubby is never far from my thoughts.

Cheers,

Sam

Chapter 15

If I've Had Four Kids, Can I Still Wear White to My Wedding?

Here comes the bride!

The great news about weddings today is that anything goes. You can wear white, even if it's your seventh marriage, or blue, even if it's your first. You can walk yourself down the aisle, walk down with your husband-to-be, or follow a parade of potbellied pigs. Small weddings are just a chic as large ones, and the best nuptials reflect the personalities and lifestyles of the couple. You can serve cupcakes or cookies instead of cake; get married in an opera house, on a boat, or in your favorite church; and pick and choose from the traditions you love and discard the ones that don't work for you as a couple.

Never before have the words "it's your day" been more true. The most important thing to remember is to make the day an expression of your personality and your love for each other. The old rules need not apply.

This Ain't the Brady Bunch

You're happy, deliriously happy, and you want to share that happiness with the world, or a least the Sunday section of your local newspaper.

One thing that is extremely important to remember is to respect the children (even if they're adult children). There's nothing more important to children than feeling that they were part of a family that wanted to be together. When you say things like, "I finally got it right," or, "I'm happy for the first time in my life," your children (or his) feel like the leftovers of a life that you wish you never had. And sometimes, in all fairness, you or your future husband do wish the children didn't exist. And they feel that.

Your new love, your marriage, feels like a clean slate to you and your partner. But the wedding is frequently when kids feel like their family has just been erased. It is truly important to practice great sensitivity.

> **"The worst day of my life was the day that my parents told me they were getting divorced. The second worst day was the day my mom got married."**
> **—Elizabeth**

All children, whether they're eighty or eight, need to believe they were born into a situation where they were loved and wanted. If you or your future husband walk around saying that your past marriage was a mistake or should never have happened, you'll be crushing the spirits of the children from the former union.

They should be happy for you, right? But sometimes children, even adult children, are so wrapped up in their own emotions they can barely deal with what they're feeling themselves, let alone conjure up a genuine smile in time for the champagne toast.

As my friend Lisa Earle McLeod likes to say, "The trickle-down theory of happiness does not work here." This new relationship may be the best thing that ever happened to you. Your first marriage may have been nineteen years of misery. You may have never been happy, and your kids may even know that.

But the best thing you can do is be respectful of their feelings.

If you are the future stepmother, you need to keep the same things in mind with your future husband's children. They may love you; they may hate you; but you and your marriage will have a much stronger chance of success if you respect the fact that his last marriage was their family.

Whether the kids are five or thirty-five, a woman can make life a whole lot easier for the children and herself if she manages their emotions on the wedding day. Why you? Because you're the one who can make the biggest difference and set the tone for the rest of the relationship. It's also important to remember that being sensitive to all of that doesn't have to take away from your happiness or the joy that you feel.

Some adult children may feel relieved after a remarriage, while younger and other adult kids may be angry, hurt, or upset. For young children, a wedding may be the final nail in the coffin— irrefutable proof that their parents aren't going to get back together.

Here are some guidelines for respecting the kids on your wedding day:

- Refrain from saying things like, "I'm happy for the first time in my life!" Even if it's true. Saying "I'm so happy!" conveys the same feelings to your friends and family without breaking anyone's heart. You can always tell your groom privately that you've never been happier.

- Ask them long before the event if they'd like to play a part in the wedding ceremony. If they say yes, let them choose how they'd like to participate. If they don't want to be involved in the ceremony, tell them you understand and respect their decision. If it's something other than what you had in mind, let it go.

- Remember, a wedding is an important ritual, but it's also just a party. Go with the flow, and if the children decide at a late hour that they can't participate in the way they'd planned to, smile, hug them, and tell them you understand.

- Remember, you set the tone for the entire family for the rest of the relationship. Make it loving, respectful, and open.

You Can't Martha Your Way to Happiness

Some women who get married after forty are trying to make up for the fact that their first wedding was not everything they'd hoped for. They march down the aisle in a virginal white dress with a cathedral train to the harmonies of a fifty-eight-member boys' choir and the gentle flapping wings of doves being released. Every pew is adorned with roses, and a formation of sixteen bridesmaids waits at the ready.

If a diamond tiara, an ice sculpture in the shape of Buckingham Palace, and a seventeen-tier cake are what you need to make your big day special, well, more power to you. But there are two things to remember: (1) there are no do-overs; and (2) there is no correlation between how fancy the wedding is and the success of the marriage. No marriage ever succeeded or failed on the basis of no-show flower girls or wrong-color napkins. I know, it's shocking. Banana fondant cannot guarantee a successful union. What is the world coming to?

Every Bride Goes Crazy Over One Thing

This is a bizarre fact of wedding planning. Some brides obsess over the perfect shoes; some obsess over vows; and some obsess over (ahem) whether or not buttercream icing should, in fact, contain butter rather than, say, vegetable shortening. This is crazy, but normal. I think your One Crazy Thing obsession is just your brain's way of dealing with the very life-changing decision in front of you—whether or not spending your life with this person is a good idea.

Frosting and strappy satin shoes are manageable disasters that keep your brain from focusing on the fact that things are about to change forever. Don't let it make you nuts.

Here Comes the Bride

In case you had any doubts, the following are answers to the most popular wedding questions I receive. This first set is answered by celebrity-wedding planner Samantha Goldberg.

Should second-time brides wear white?

Many years ago, the traditional white dress signified the bride had been with no other man. It meant she was pure and giving herself only to her husband, and he would be the only man in her life through sickness and health, etc. Unfortunately, there is no guarantee when you get married that it is going to last a lifetime; however, we would like to hope that it will. Whether this is a first marriage, second, third, or eighth, the etiquette is that you wear what you want. There are even brides nowadays that do not want to wear a wedding dress at all. I had a client who was marrying for the third time, and she had a gown made in a light shade of pink. It had a beautiful train and veil, and it was what she wanted. Just because a bride has worn white once does not mean she should not wear a white dress again; she is still a bride in the eyes of her husband-to-be!

Who gives the bride away if she's fifty?

If a bride is lucky enough to have healthy parents, she can choose to have her father or a close male friend do it, or she may walk halfway down the aisle alone and meet her groom there. They can walk together towards the altar. All very sentimental, and again, no right or wrong answer.

Is it tacky to accept gifts?

If a couple is very established, they may not need household items, and it's quite all right to note on the invitation, "The gift of your presence is all that is hoped for."

Some may register for particular items they will use as a "new couple," like stemware. A few of my clients have asked their guests to donate to a specific medical charity, like heart disease or Alzheimer's, especially if one or more of their parents was affected by the disease. A special bottle of wine or a homemade gift reflecting the couples hobbies or tastes is quite common and welcome.

What is the biggest misconception about marrying at this stage?

That the couple or person should be waiting a longer time to have a relationship. I knew a wonderful couple who got married last year. Both of their significant others had passed away around the same time—six months prior to their meeting. They met, and five months later, they were engaged. She told me it was like her deceased husband wanted her to find him. They both had children, and somehow everything just worked—no resentment of moving on from the children. It just felt right. You saw where the phrase "soul mates" rang true in this particular relationship.

What is the biggest faux pas?

Some will say inviting your ex to the wedding. It may be perceived as a mixed message that the person is not healing and moving on. In the end, only you know what's best for you in this new chapter as man and wife.

Tara Null, a destination wedding planner and owner of Fiestas Los Cabos (www.fiestasloscabos.com) gives the inside scoop for brides over forty.

What are the biggest differences between younger brides and brides over forty?

Older brides are more decisive and more confident. They know what they want, and they trust me. They know their budget; they know exactly what kind of flowers they want; they have their colors or theme picked out; and they're more confident in their decisions.

Who pays?

The bride and groom normally pay for the wedding (this is true for most brides over thirty). If it's a first wedding for the bride, the parents pay about half the time; the bride and groom pay the other half of the time.

Do over-forty brides and grooms still want a traditional wedding?

They still want the traditional wedding—a lot of them still wear traditional wedding gowns. We still get white and ivory dresses. Brides are not wearing a lot of colored dresses.

When they're a little older, most of the time they have more money, and they can do things they didn't do the first time. They have more flowers, fireworks, or fire dancers.

How should you deal with all the assorted families?

A destination wedding makes it harder for the exes to come. Kids are usually involved in a traditional way—by doing a reading or, if they're younger, being a flower girl, ring bearer, or junior attendant.

It's really important for all brides to tell their coordinator what the family dynamics are: We need to know if your mom and dad hate each other, or if your two sisters don't get along or if your sister just got divorced. I once asked the very recently separated sister of the bride to dance with her husband; she started bawling and ran out of the room.

We had a bride once who truly hated her mom—she didn't want to have her in the dressing room, didn't want her involved in any way—but she didn't tell us until the wedding day. If you let us know what the family dynamics are ahead of time, we can run interference for you, watch what we say, and accommodate, or at the very least, refrain from making, any requests or toasts that might send someone running to the ladies' room for a tissue. Even if it's embarrassing, it works far better to let us know ahead of time.

Yours, Mine, and the Battle of Wills—Things to Consider Before You Tie the Knot

It's far more complicated to get married once you've amassed assets and responsibilities. Be sure to nail down these answers before you take the next step, and have your wishes legally documented.

- How will your children and his children be provided for?

- How will you or your spouse be provided for in the event of death or divorce?

- If one of you passes away before the other, who keeps the house?

- What family heirlooms are you planning to leave to your children and not your spouse?

Conclusion

The Party's Just Getting Started

Well, now we've come to the end of the book, the beginning of the next chapter of your life.

Are love and dating different than they were when you were twenty or thirty? You bet. But knowing (and being comfortable with) who you are and what you have to offer can make your relationships deeper, sweeter, and more fulfilling.

I hope you realize what a wonderful, amazing woman you are. I also hope you know that you deserve to find the kind of relationship you've been hoping for. The first step is in *knowing* you deserve it.

Keep the faith, and trust me: You deserve it all.

I'm pulling for you.

—Lisa

If you have questions that were not answered in this book or you'd like to drop me a line, find about more about something I mentioned in the book, or send me a personal question, please contact me at www. lisadaily.com. I'd love to hear from you.

Resources

Daytime is a nationally syndicated morning TV show. www.daytimeonline.TV

Wendy Allen, MA, is a certified feng shui consultant and trainer, as well as an art therapist and psychotherapist.

Dr. Gary Alter is a Beverly Hills plastic surgeon and assistant clinical professor of plastic surgery at UCLA.

Michael Alvear is the host of HBO's *Sex Inspectors* and creator of Blabbermash.com.

Mark Amtower, is the founder of Amtower and Company, author of *Government Marketing Best Practices,* and widely regarded as a leading expert in marketing to the federal government.

Dr. Myra Belgeri is an associate professor at the St. Louis College of Pharmacy.

Dr. Marianne Dainton is a communication professor and assistant department chair at La Salle University.

Laura Davimes is a researcher, herbalist, educator, and aromatherapy expert. She is the owner of Herban Avenues, and creator of the Man-Magnet Parfum Glacé. www.herbanavenues.com

Leatrice Eiseman is director of the Pantone Color Institute. She heads the Eiseman Center for Color Information and Training, and has been called "America's color guru."
   www.colorexpert.com/about.html

Mary Jo Fay is the author of *Please Dear, Not Tonight: The Truth about Women and Sex* and is a national speaker on narcissism.

Jan Dahlin Geiger is a certified financial planner and author of *Get Your Assets in Gear! Smart Money Strategies.*

Samantha Goldberg is a wedding and events coordinator on the Style Network and the host of *It's Your Wedding* on the Wedding Podcast Network.

Gregory Hartley is a former Army interrogator and co-author of *How to Spot a Liar.*

Christopher Hopkins is the author of *Staging Your Comeback: A Complete Beauty Revival for Women Over 45* and is known as the Makeover Guy on *Oprah.*
   www.themakeoverguy.com

Kidder Kaper is the Internet radio host of *Sex Is Fun!*

Anne Kreamer is the author of *Going Gray: What I Learned About Beauty, Sex, Work, Motherhood, Authenticity and Everything Else That Really Matters,* co-developer of *Spy* magazine, and creator of *Nickelodeon* magazine.
   www.annekreamer.com

Dion McInnis is a photographer and author of *Listen to Life: Wisdom in Life's Stories.* He celebrates all people in images and words.
   www.dionmcinnis.com

Lisa Earle McLeod is an inspirational humorist, expert on human angst, syndicated newspaper columnist, and author of *Forget Perfect* and *Finding Grace When You Can't Even Find Clean Underwear.*

www.forgetperfect.com

Dr. Albert Mehrabian is a spatial psychologist and professor emeritus of Psychology at UCLA. He speaks at seminars worldwide on human communication and his "7%-38%-55% Rule."

Tara Null is a destination-wedding planner.

www.fiestasloscabos.com

Tina Puente is an advertising, marketing, and public relations consultant and the creator of hiretina.com.

www.hiretina.com

Wayne Schaffel is the president of the Public Relations Network and has worked with Fortune 500 Companies.

www.prforless.com

Robert Siciliano is CEO of IDTheftSecurity.com and author of *The Safety Minute: 01.* He is an identity-theft expert and speaker on personal security.

www.IDTheftSecurity.com

Jennifer Weiner is the best-selling author of *Good in Bed.*

www.jenniferweiner.com

Patti Wood is a speaker, author, and body-language expert who has been written up in the *New York Times.*

www.pattiwood.net

Dating sites that cater to the over-forty crowd:

Lavalife Prime (www.prime.lavalife.com)

Match.com

YourTimeSingles.com

Cupid.com

SeniorFriendFinder.com

Niche dating sites:

eHarmony.com (marriage-minded singles)

CatholicSingles.com

RepublicanSingles.us

Democratsingles.com

JDate.com (caters to Jewish singles but has a large base of non-Jewish New York City singles as well)

General dating sites:

PlentyofFish.com (largest online site, free to members)

Match.com

Lavalife.com

Cupid.com

Online dating site tool to help you choose the best site for you based on your dating goals:

www.LisaDaily.com

Enter the code GROWNUP to use the tool for free.

Speed-dating sites:

PreDating.com (largest speed-dating company in the United States with events in most cities; dates are about four to six minutes, so you'll meet around twenty to twenty-five people during one two- to three-hour event)

8minutedating.com (fewer dates for a longer time—eight minutes)

Fastdater.com (three-minute dates, so you'll meet about forty people in one night)

SpeedDating.com (original speed-dating company; caters to Jewish singles)

Classmate search sites:

Classmates.com

Reunion.com

FindClassmatesForFree.com

Date ideas to get you out of the theater:

Habitat for Humanity (habitat.org)

DanceNet (havetodance.com)

Wallbounce.com

Greatamericandays.com

Totalexperience.ca

Singles vacations:

SinglesCruises.com

Safety:

MyPrivateLine.com (for a fee, company provides a disposable number for people to call you, which can be forwarded to your home or cell)

Acknowledgments

I am so thankful to all of the people who made *How to Date Like a Grown-Up* a labor of love.

First, thanks to my sweet and fantastic husband, Tom, who is exactly the sort of man I'd always hoped for and was delighted to find really exists. Thanks to my Quinn and Elle, for being charming and sweet and inspiring and an endless source of entertainment. Thanks to my mom for her constant support, cheerleading, and enthusiasm, for stepping in while I traveled, and being such a wonderful friend. I am blessed to have all of you in my life.

Thanks to our family, especially the women who inspire me, make me laugh, and mix a mean batch of guacamole: my Aunt Jerry, Mary, Steph, Lizzy, and Cassie—all of the Parks women past, present, and future.

Thanks to the Debutantes and the John Grisham Coffee Club (otherwise known as Mid-listers Anonymous) for making life as an author possible for extreme extroverts.

Thanks to Lisa Earle McLeod, my best friend, my frequent and favorite writing partner, and author of *Forget Perfect; Finding Grace When You Can't Even Find Clean Underwear;* and the book that will change the world, the *Triangle of Truth*. I take full credit for all of her best work, as she, rightfully, takes full credit for mine. Thanks to our husbands (and children) for being so patient with our nine-calls-a-day phone habit.

Love to Michael Alvear, my favorite TV star (*Sex Inspectors*) and the hilarious author of *Men Are Pigs but We Love Bacon, Sex Inspectors,* and *Alexander the Fabulous.*

Thanks to Susan Harrow, media-coaching genius and author of *Sell Yourself Without Selling Your Soul,* who has turned me into a sound-bite maven and has me prepped and ready to roll for *Oprah.* (Just in case they were wondering.)

Thanks to my fabulous agent, Jenny Bent, for being such an extraordinary matchmaker and all-around genius. Thanks to my brilliant and gifted editor, Shana Drehs, who was endlessly patient as I foolishly attempted to tour and write a book at the same time. A million thanks to the entire Sourcebooks team for their enthusiasm and hard work, and to our brilliant cover designer, Dawn Pope, whose elegant and beautiful design made me swoon. Big thanks to Heather Moore and Carrie Gellin for their hard work and for being the best-organized PR team I've ever met.

Thanks to my TV family at *Daytime*—Cyndi, Dave, Coleen, Maureen, Marci, Jen, April, Rob, the other Rob, Jill, Ben, and resident mystery man, Steve—you guys are great. Big thanks to the crew—you're the best!

Thanks to Kitty Etherly, magician and truly gifted publicist. You are extraordinarily talented and a delight to work with.

Thanks to the brilliant Eric Straus and everyone at Cupid/PreDating.com. Thanks to the TR girls: Susan, Heidi, Seanna, Angela, Rebecca, Jennifer, Tessa, Laura, Iris, and all the rest—the biggest reason why Sarasota is the most fabulous place we've ever lived.

Thanks to Ashley, my über-efficient and brilliant assistant, world traveler, and super-fun traveling companion. This year would not have been possible without you.

A big thanks to Laura Davimes of Herban Avenues, who created the scintillating Dreamgirl Man-Magnet Parfum Glacé just for me. It's my favorite. And Tom's.

And last, thanks to my readers and the thousands of self-made dreamgirls and dreamgirls-in-training who have written or shown up to Dreamgirl Academy events—I thank you from the bottom of my heart. You are the reason I do what I do, and I have my fingers crossed for each and every one of you.

About the Author

Lisa Daily is the relationship expert on *Daytime,* a nationally syndicated morning TV show; a syndicated columnist; and the author of *Stop Getting Dumped!* and *Fifteen Minutes of Shame.* www.lisadaily.com

*Some letters have been edited for clarity.